Raymond Mitchell was born in Newcastle upon Tyne in 1920. He matriculated from Heaton Grammar School and obtained a clerical post with the City Engineer's Department in 1937. In 1940 he volunteered for the Royal Marines and after initial training served in the 8th Battalion as Orderly Room clerk and then motorcyclist in the Carrier Platoon. He was with 41 Commando from its inception in 1942 and saw action in the Mediterranean Theatre as a rifleman and afterwards in north-west Europe, as a despatch rider, from D-Day to the end of the war.

Back in civilian life in 1946, he continued a career in engineering, becoming a Chartered Civil Engineer and Chartered Municipal Engineer in 1952. Raymond Mitchell retired in 1985 from the position of Assistant City Engineer of Newcastle. He lives in High Heaton.

Dedicated to the Memory of

Po/X 105922 Marine ALEC KENNEDY of Glasgow
Q Troop, No. 41 Royal Marines Commando

Killed in Action at Salerno, 10 September 1943

MARINE COMMANDO

Sicily and Salerno, 1943
with 41 Royal Marines Commando

Raymond Mitchell

ROBERT HALE · LONDON

© *Raymond Mitchell 1988*
First published in Great Britain 1988
This paperback edition 1994

Robert Hale Limited
Clerkenwell House
Clerkenwell Green
London EC1R 0HT

ISBN 0-7090-5585-4

The author and publisher would like to thank Eric Morris and Century Hutchinson Ltd for permission to quote from *Salerno – A Military Fiasco* by Eric Morris.

1   3   5   7   9   10   8   6   4   2

Printed and bound in Malta
by Interprint Limited

Contents

Illustrations

Picture credits

6-16: courtesy of the Imperial War Museum. All other photographs supplied by the author.

Abbreviations

ADS	Advanced Dressing Station
AMGOT	Allied Military Government of Occupied Territories
ANZAC	Australian and New Zealand Army Corps – formed during World War I, they greatly distinguished themselves in the Dardanelles campaign
CB	Confined to Barracks. A military punishment which included extra duties, extra drill and frequent reporting to the guardroom
CCS	Casualty Clearing Station
CGH	Canadian General Hospital
CO	Commanding Officer
D-Day	The first day of any planned military operation. Now generally interpreted as 6 June 1944 – the first day of the biggest one of all – the Allied invasion of Europe
DID	Divisional Issuing Depot – The 'quartermaster's store' of an Army Division of 17-18,000 men
DUKW	Factory code letters of General Motors, D – 1942, U – Utility (Amphibian), K – All-wheel drive, W – Dual rear axles. American amphibious vehicle capable of carrying 30 armed men or 2½ tons of supplies at 50 mph on land or 5 mph in water. Not unnaturally known as 'DUCKS', they were first used in the Sicily landings
EY	EmergencY. The 'EY' was a standard infantry rifle, reinforced with a wire binding, for use in

	hurling hand grenades. So named because it was to be used with ball ammunition only in an emergency
FDL	Forward Defended Locality – the 'front line'
H-Hour	The precise timing of the initial main assault of any attack
LCA	Landing Craft, Assault
LCI(S)	Landing Craft, Infantry, Small
LCT	Landing Craft, Tank
LMG	Light Machine Gun
MDS	Main Dressing Station
NAAFI	Navy, Army and Air Forces' Institute. A civilian organization which provides canteen, etc., facilities for the armed forces
OP	Observation Post
RAMC	Royal Army Medical Corps
RAP	Regimental Aid Post
RTU	Return to Unit. For Army commandos (who were all volunteers from other units) this was a death sentence so far as any further commando service was concerned
SBA	Sick-Berth Attendant
SP	Self-Propelled (gun)
TCV	Troop-Carrying Vehicle
2 i/c	Second-in-Command
TSMG	Thompson Sub-Machine-Gun (tommy gun)

HO	Hostilities Only	
CS	Continuous Service	} types of marine service

BD	Battledress	
KSD	Khaki Service Dress	} types of uniform

Foreword
by
Colonel J.F. Parsons OBE MC RM

Raymond Mitchell gives a marine's eye view of the operations of 41 Commando in Sicily and at Salerno and it is good that he has done so because, in the final analysis, it is the marine who wins the battle. Mitchell graphically describes the confusion and 'the fog of war' which always descends over the battlefield. This was never more so than at Salerno because of the closeness of the country which limited visibility and, because so many of the officers and NCOs became casualties the word was not always passed down. It is then that courage, determination and self-discipline really count. This and comradeship keep a marine going. It is always relatively easy for an officer or NCO to be brave because the spotlight is on him and he has his responsibilities. But the marine has just himself, his training and his mates.

Sicily and Salerno marked the serious return of the Royal Marines to the Commando business, a role which had traditionally been theirs for over 300 years but which had been assumed by the Army when, at the beginning of the war, the Corps was fully committed to providing a Royal Marines Division.

In Sicily and Salerno the Commando was lightly equipped for a primarily raiding role. There were no 'big companies' or elaborate command systems. The Commanding Officer personally led six Fighting Troops, each of about seventy men and each led by a young officer – a captain. The Commando carried all it needed on its back or, as when going forward to lay anti-tank mines, draped around the neck, and had but a single truck at Headquarters. Close personal leadership at all levels was the secret of success. The Commando fought with dash and won by surprise and by doing the seemingly impossible.

Later in the war it became clear that, if Commandos were to make the most effective contribution to the land battle, they must be prepared and equipped to remain committed ashore for more protracted periods and so their organization became heavier and their anti-tank capability strengthened. But the ability of Royal Marine Commandos to operate fast, to carry very heavy loads and to surprise the enemy by attacking from an unexpected direction or by night remains, as was so well demonstrated in the recent Falklands Campaign.

Raymond Mitchell has written a very good account of a proud chapter in the history of the Royal Marines and I think it will bring pleasure to many.

John Parsons

Colonel Parsons won his Military Cross at Salerno as a Troop Commander with 41 Commando and continued his service with various Royal Marines Commando Units and other formations. His last appointment was as Commanding Officer, Infantry Training, Royal Marines from 1967 to 1969, when he was appointed ADC to Her Majesty the Queen. He retired from the Corps in 1970.

Author's Preface

During World War II it was an offence to keep a diary whilst on active service, lest it fell into the wrong hands and divulged useful information to the enemy. Nevertheless, when released from the Royal Marines in 1946, after more than five years' service, I had an assortment of notes and other factual material covering most of that time with the Corps and an unformulated conviction that, eventually, they would all be arranged into a coherent whole. I made a start immediately on returning home but soon had to put the work to one side in order to concentrate upon studying for professional qualifications as a civil engineer.

When writing re-started, it proceeded spasmodically, having to give way to the higher priorities of work, marriage and raising a family. I had hoped to be ready should any of the children ever ask, 'What did you do in the war, Daddy?', but as the process of arranging, enlarging, explaining and describing proceeded by fits and starts, it became apparent that they would all be grown up before any part had been completed. It was only after my retirement that sufficient time became available to finalize this episode.

The book is restricted in scope, as it deals only with the Mediterranean period of 41 Commando, and also in content, by concentrating upon the recollections of a single marine. Within those confines, however, it is a genuine attempt to present a complete picture. Everyone else who was involved will have another story to tell, similar in outline but different in detail, as only a very small part of any action can be seen from a single firing-position. Then, apart from the foxholes, the bombs and the bullets, there were fruitless patrols and incongruous interludes, mess decks and rest areas, compo rations, flies and dysentery – more mundane matters but still important parts of that whole that couldn't be left out.

A great deal more could be written about the Commando's part in the Sicily and Salerno operations: details of the officers and men involved, casualties suffered, decorations awarded, and some part of this can be found in Eric Morris's book *Salerno* (Hutchinson, 1983). But, if anyone has picked up this volume thinking, 'At last! – a book about 41!' I apologize – that book has yet to be written. The Mediterranean was just the beginning of 41's battle experience. Any history of the Commando would go on to include D-Day with the British Second Army, the Normandy beachhead, the pursuit through North-West Europe with the Canadian First Army, the landing on the Dutch island of Walcheren to open the port of Antwerp, and risky operations on the River Maas, before subsequent duties in Germany. Then there would be a completely new section dealing with the Korean War.

I am indebted to Corporal (later Sergeant) 'Jan' Maley, acting section sergeant at Salerno, for reading an early draft and putting me right on a few important points of detail. Also to Marine Harry Weiss, Q Troop sniper, for his assistance on a more recent version. My thanks too to Joan and 'Cas' Castiaux, Ivor Johnson and Jim Murray for their very helpful comments on the readability and comprehension of the text. A lot of credit must also go to my wife, Joan, for her continuing support and the many hours she spent in typing and re-typing early drafts in the days before word-processors.

1 *Off at Last*

Monday 28 June 1943 was a hot summer's day. From a cloudless blue sky, the sun shimmered on the calm waters of the Firth of Clyde and beat down upon the crowded decks of a score of fully laden troopships lying at anchor within sight of Gourock. Plumes of black smoke, curling from their funnels in the light breeze, showed that they all had steam up and were ready for sea.

One of the group was the 35,000 ton liner SS *Durban Castle*, now equipped for war service as an Infantry Landing Ship, with rows of blunt-nosed LCAs (Landing Craft Assault) ranged high along her tall sides. Amongst the many hundreds of troops packed on board, and fully trained in the use of these small craft, was No. 41 Royal Marines Commando under the command of Lieutenant-Colonel B.J.D. Lumsden RM. One of the riflemen in Q Troop of the Commando was CH/X 100977 Marine Raymond Mitchell, author of these memoirs.

The Commando had been formed the previous October at Llanion Barracks, Pembroke Dock, South Wales – base depot of the Royal Welch Fusiliers. It had arisen phoenix-like from the ashes of the 8th Battalion, Royal Marines, when all suitable men were selected for commando training. This began a few days later, after the unit had moved to the south of England, and continued for the next six months, first at Weymouth, then on and around the Isle of Wight. There had also been periods at the Commando Training Centre, based upon Achnacarry House, near Spean Bridge, Scotland, and the Street Fighting School in West Ham, London, where a few acres of bomb-blasted housing provided a realistic urban battleground.

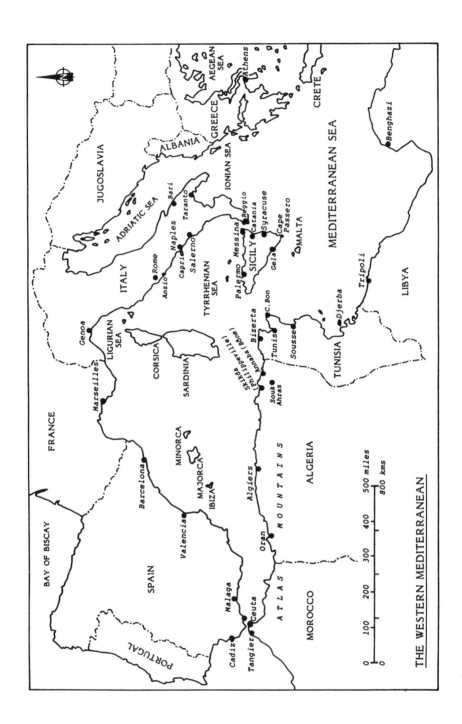

THE WESTERN MEDITERRANEAN

At the beginning of April the Commando had left the Isle of Wight and entrained for an eighteen-hour mystery tour which landed us at Troon, the golfing resort on the Ayrshire coast of Scotland. There, as usual, we were billeted in civilian homes – an integral part of the commando training system, designed to cultivate a sense of independence and self-reliance. The parquet floors of the Moncrieff residence on Bentinck Drive were unaccustomed to heavy army boots but Jack Horsfield and I were made welcome. Rigorous training sessions continued and we soon found ourselves repeating the same pattern of night speed marches which suggested that the Commando was already rehearsing the basic manœuvres of a specific operation for which it had been earmarked.

Q Troop's office was housed in vacant shop premises, next door to Forte's ice-cream parlour. It was there that, on the morning of 14 June, we had paraded in 'embarkation order and small kitbags'. Our sea bags, the type normally used by 'blue marines' when they joined their ships, were already stacked in the back room of the shop where they had been dumped the previous day. Commandos were 'khaki marines', wearing standard army battledress but distinguishable by their green berets, 'Royal Marines Commando' shoulder flashes and the Combined Operations badge worn on their sleeves. Those large bags of ours contained the kit, including best battledress, greatcoat and winter woollies, which was to be left behind in the UK.

We had marched to Troon railway station for the journey to Gourock, about forty miles away, and were soon on board a small vessel, bobbing about amongst a fleet of troopships anchored in the Firth of Clyde. They already seemed fully laden; the rails far above our heads were lined with boisterous soldiers for whom the progress of our lowly vessel was a welcome diversion. Steaming along the length of ship after ship, we ran the gauntlet of barrages of cheerful, if largely unprintable, banter bawled down upon us from a great height until our craft approached what was obviously *our* ship. The sallyport doors in her side were open wide, and a group of crew members stood by to receive us.

The *Durban Castle* – we read the name on her lifebelts as we climbed aboard – appeared to be already loaded to capacity, yet the whole Commando of some 500 officers and men was absorbed into the bowels of the ship without seeming to make any noticeable impression upon the mass of humanity already in occupation. Most of them were Canadians whose shoulder flashes we recognized from a previous encounter: the 'Princess Pats' (Princess Patricia's Canadian Light Infantry, from Winnipeg and Vancouver) and the Edmonton Regiment (more properly the Edmonton, West Nova Scotia, Royal 22nd, a battalion of French-Canadians from Quebec Province). Only a few weeks earlier, the Commando had shared a muddy, rain-sodden camp at Inveraray with those two units. The intention had been to carry out joint landing excercises on the shores of Loch Fyne but gale-force winds had made conditions much too rough for small craft. We spent most of our time there cowering in doorways on a deserted dockside, trying to shelter from the lashing rain. Maybe this time together we would have better weather.

One thing hadn't changed: it was still necessary to tread very carefully when passing through the Canadian enclaves, to thread your way around the innumerable groups of men squatting on the deck, 'shooting craps'. It must have been the same throughout the convoy, as the entire Canadian First Division, of almost 18,000 men, with all their tanks, guns and stores, was already housed on board those anchored ships.

During the two weeks since joining her, the *Durban Castle* hadn't strayed far from the waters of the Clyde. There had been a number of false alarms when sudden departures for the open sea had us thinking that we were on our way – only to find that it had been no more than a cruise around the Isle of Arran, from which we were soon making a leisurely return to anchorage.

Shore leave had been non-existent but the Commandos were privileged to make two short expeditions on Scottish soil. Officially, these landings were to keep us in training by stretching leg muscles with a route march but in actuality their purpose was to do the weekly wash in the soft water of a lowland burn. On shipboard, only a mile or so from the shore, the use of fresh water for any purpose other than cooking and drinking was strictly forbidden. Sea water had to be used for all forms of washing, including clothes and persons, and notwithstanding the use of the much-vaunted sea-water soap, it was never possible to obtain more than a meagre lather.

The days passed slowly, and after a week or so it was generally accepted that this time it was 'for keeps' – but there were still some sceptics. After all, we had been through the entire procedure more than once before. Only a fortnight previously we had made the same journey to Gourock, embarked upon a troopship, carried out similar cruises in Scottish waters but, after five days, found ourselves back in Troon as if nothing had happened.

Then the Commando was required to make another trip ashore, which confirmed that this time there would be no return to billets. Deep in a pine forest, Lord Louis Mountbatten, Chief of Combined Operations, addressed us from the bonnet of a jeep, expressing his regret that he had to stay behind in Britain and wishing us Godspeed. The time had come to write 'last letters'.

On that Monday in June, when the whole convoy had steam up ready for sea, Frank Barker and I were 'cooks' for No. 127 mess. This didn't involve any actual cooking: the job was no more than collecting meals from the galley, sharing out the food as equally as possible, perhaps slightly more equal for ourselves, returning the trays and cleaning up afterwards. In view of the immense number of men on board, all meals were served on a fixed rota basis, as and when ready, so a lot of the cooks' time was spent in just hanging around outside the serving hatches, waiting for their particular mess number to be called. When the first throbs of the ship's engines signalled our imminent departure from the Clyde, Frank and I were standing in line for the issue of the evening meal. Any thoughts about gripping the ship's rail for a misty-eyed farewell were pointless: we had no alternative but to stay in the queue until someone bawled out '1-2-7!'

Few had any regrets about leaving the UK. After many

months of training, in Battalion and Commando, then the previous two weeks of floating around in a limbo between Scotland and the deep blue sea, the general feeling was one of relief that we were, at last, actually going somewhere. No one seemed very much concerned about just where that somewhere might be, but there was no shortage of guesses. 'South of France – here we come!' some wag called out. 'Greece, more like,' came another. 'How d'ye fancy Japland?' 'Bet it's Italy' – and many more besides. For two weeks we had been bombarded with so many and varied rumours ('buzzes' in Marine parlance) that we were rather punch-drunk with the whole business and were just pleased to be getting into things.

The serving position where Frank and I were standing was in the recreation space on A Deck. It was fitted with large 'observation'-type windows, but from our place in the queue, we could see no more than the tops of the Ayrshire hills slipping slowly away behind us. As we watched, rather mesmerized, someone in the rowdy throng started to whistle the tune of that well-worn barrack-room ballad:

> We don't know where we're going till we're there.
> There are lots and lots of rumours in the air.
> I heard the captain say, 'We're on the move today' –
> I only hope the blinking sergeant-major knows the way!

By the time we had collected the meal, served it, cleared up and made our way onto an upper deck for a breath of fresh air, it was dusk. The convoy was well out at sea, steaming steadily southwards, with the coast of Scotland no more than a purplish smudge on our port beam. We could not have been very far from that part of the smudge which was Troon. Were there already strange feet under *my* table, I wondered.

One thing at least *was* beyond any doubt – that, wherever bound, we were certainly 'on the move today'!

2 Steaming Towards the Mediterranean

It wasn't until the third day out that we were given any indication of our destination. Then, after a prior warning to 'Stand by loudspeakers at noon', we heard the captain of the ship announce, 'You are sailing to the Mediterranean to take part in the greatest Combined Operation of all time ...' His voice was drowned in an outburst of cheers, whistles and shouts of 'France!' 'Greece!' 'Italy!' At least the field of speculation had been considerably reduced. The captain's announcement was followed by personal messages from Lord Louis Mountbatten, the Admiral of the Convoy (Rear-Admiral Vian who, as captain of HMS *Cossack*, had rescued the *Graf Spee*'s merchant navy prisoners from the *Altmark* in January 1940) and Major-General Guy Simonds, Commanding General of the First Canadian Division, but none of them disclosed any further information.

Two more days passed in pointless conjecture until, at the conclusion of boat drill on the fifth day out, our Troop Commander, Captain Stott, announced that the Colonel was to address the whole Commando and led the way to the Canadian dining-saloon. When all Troops had been assembled (the whole place was buzzing like an overturned beehive), the adjutant called for order with the command 'Sit to attention', and in strode Colonel (Bertie) Lumsden, with a broad grin of anticipation on his face. He knew very well that there was only one question flying around in all those hundreds of heads arranged before him, 'Where? ... Where?? ... WHERE???' He came straight

19

to the point. 'We are to take part in the invasion of Italy – through Sicily!'

His words unleashed a pandemonium of cheers, catcalls and whoops of delight against a background babble of 'Italy ... Sicily ... Italy ... Sicily'. Heads turned towards neighbours, and eyes searched out particular friends at a distance, to verify that they fully appreciated what had been said. Yells of 'What did I tell you?' 'Didn't I say ...' 'I thought it would be ...' shot back and forth. An announcement of fourteen days' leave could hardly have created a greater furore. For a full minute, while our brains were absorbing the fact of finally knowing where we were headed, the Colonel stood with arms folded across his chest talking quietly to Major McCann, his second-in-command. When the uproar had subsided slightly, he raised his hand and we all quietened down to listen in attentive silence while he proceeded to 'put us in the picture'.

We learned that our convoy, large as it was, carried only a small part of the total invasion forces. The American Seventh Army was also at sea, sailing direct from the United States, heading for the south coast of Sicily, where it would land on the broad beaches of the Bay of Gela. Then, at the appropriate time, the British Eighth Army, to which we and the Canadian First Division now belonged, would sail from North Africa to play its part in the overall plan. Our convoy was headed for the south-eastern corner of Sicily – to the vicinity of Cape Passero, some seventy miles east of the American landing. The Canadians were to attack to the west of the cape while the main body of the Eighth Army would go ashore at various points on the east coast of Sicily extending as far north as Syracuse.

The specific ships of the Royal Navy that would be on hand to take care of the Italian fleet as the convoys neared their respective landfalls were made known to us, and it was also of some comfort to learn that the overall air support to be provided for the invasion would outnumber the entire German Luftwaffe. It was also revealed that since leaving the UK our convoy had steamed far into the Atlantic in an attempt to mislead the enemy as to our true destination but was executing a wide sweep that would bring us to the Straits of Gibraltar in a few days' time. Also in the convoy was our sister unit, No. 40 Commando, which had taken part in the Dieppe raid the previous year, now under the command of Lieutenant-Colonel J.C. Manners. The Commando Brigade made up of these two units would be the first sea-borne troops to go ashore to initiate the long-awaited return to Europe of Allied Armies. The brigade's initial task would be to neutralize enemy coastal strongpoints that could threaten the Canadian landing; then, for the next two or three days, it would protect the Canadian left flank while they were getting their men and materials ashore and pushing forward to link up with the main body of the Eighth Army. When the Canadians had no further need of us, No. 41 Commando was to be based on two assault ships as a floating striking force ready to undertake further landings at short notice.

After the earlier complete lack of information, the sudden flood was almost too much to assimilate all at once, and when we were dismissed, most heads were reeling with a form of mental indigestion.

During the following days we spent long periods in the operations room, studying maps and aerial photographs. The overall invasion plan was for the Americans to cross Sicily in a straight thrust towards the northern coast, and capture the port of Palermo, thus effectively cutting the island in two, while the British and Canadian forces would strike up the east coast through Catania to the Straits of Messina. After the capture of Palermo, the Americans would also head towards Messina to join the British and Canadians in squeezing the enemy into the top right-hand corner of the island.

We were given the latest intelligence about the deployment of enemy forces on the island, which were estimated to amount to some six or seven divisions, mainly Italian. Some of these were 'known to be first-line troops' but others had been classed as 'second-rate garrison troops'. The efficiency of these latter formations, we were assured, was '... expected to diminish by about sixty per cent if forced to leave their defensive positions' – which was encouraging, if rather vague. The stretch of coast we were going to attack was defended by the Napoli Division (recruited, as the name indicates, from the vicinity of Naples), but there was no information about their likely fighting qualities. A German armoured division was known to be based in the island but it was anticipated that the initial jobs of the Commando Brigade would have been long accomplished before it could be brought into action.

The Canadian Division, going ashore on the western coast of the Cape Passero peninsula, would in effect be going in by the back door, in relation to the main forces of the Eighth Army landing on the east coast of the island. The wide, curving beach chosen for the operation lies some six miles from the small town of Pachino, which was to be their first objective. During the night of the invasion, Pachino was to be visited at intervals by the RAF in the hope that the enemy would be directing his eyes skywards rather than towards the coast and that the approach of our task force would, therefore, go unnoticed. The town possessed a tall water-tower (which constituted the only distinctive feature in an otherwise flat landscape), and it would provide an ideal aiming mark for the Canadian attack – so the RAF bomber crews were to be instructed to leave it standing.

The major disadvantage of the chosen landing beach was that at its western end it was overlooked, and so commanded, by a headland, the Punta Castellazzo, on which it was known that there was an Italian strongpoint. The primary requirement of the Commando attack was to ensure that this enemy position had been put out of action before the Canadians started to go ashore. The Commando Brigade was to make its touchdown in a smaller bay on the opposite side of the Punta from the Canadians' beach, and this was given the code-name of 'Commando Cove'.

Using detailed maps of the area, the overall objective was broken down into specific tasks for the two Commandos. No. 41 was to go ashore first, and after securing the beachhead it would move eastwards, towards Punta Castellazzo. No. 40 would land ten minutes later to widen the attacking front, pass through the beachhead, then swing along the coast in the opposite direction, towards Solarino. When No. 41 had achieved its first objective of safeguarding the Canadian landings, we were to move inland, to a ridge of high ground some two miles from the coast, and dig in, ready to hold off any counter-attack that might develop. During the initial period of clearing the beach area and setting up our defensive position in the hills, speed would be essential if our objectives were to be achieved before the enemy could react strongly, so no prisoners were to be taken as this would slow us down, and in any case we wouldn't have any spare men to look after them.

In addition to the Punta Castellazzo in the east, the stretch of coastline near Commando Cove was also dominated at its western end by another headland, the Punta Ciriga. Commando Cove itself, judging from aerial photographs, was enclosed by steep cliffs some thirty feet high and, although the beach looked invitingly flat, there was no information as to whether or not it had been mined. Beyond the cliffs the oblique photographs showed an attractive, gently rising hinterland of what we assumed to be vineyards and olive groves, dotted with brilliantly white farm buildings and houses. British Military Intelligence maps, however, showed many of these to be part of the coastal defences and had identified them as gun-emplacements, strong-points and barracks.

As the task of securing the beachhead would involve the marines in crossing an open beach, which could be mined, and climbing those cliffs, quite likely under a cross-fire from two fortified headlands, before even getting to grips with the enemy, a 'sticky' landing was anticipated. Likely casualties of the order of fifty per cent were glibly talked about and had apparently been accepted – at least by the higher echelons of command. Our views weren't solicited. Consequently, all operations subsequent to the establishment of the beachhead were worked out on the assumption that they would have to be carried out with greatly depleted numbers of men.

At one stage it was suggested that, after hitting the beach, one Troop – Q had been chosen – should remain in their landing-craft to engage the enemy positions, drawing their fire, while the remainder of the Commando crossed the beach and scaled the cliffs. We were not greatly enamoured of this suggestion, so it was a substantial relief when the idea was eventually dropped. One of the basic precepts of carrying out a landing on an enemy coast is 'GET OFF THE BEACH'. The enemy, after all, knows precisely where his own beach is, so he can throw all sorts of stuff onto it – and onto you too, if you happen to be there, so you don't hang around: you get away from the beach just as fast as you can.

The Commando task was then broken down into Troop objectives. A Marine Commando at that time consisted of a Headquarters Troop and six Fighting Troops, each of the latter being identified by letters of the alphabet, in our case, A, B, P, Q, X and Y. The Headquarters Troop was the organizational core of the unit and, as well as the colonel, second-in-command, adjutant and padre, included a medical officer with his sick-berth personnel, an intelligence section and a signals section. It also housed a large part of the total fire-power of the Commando in the 'heavy weapons' section, which handled our two Vickers heavy machine-guns and two three-inch mortars; later in the war it was expanded into a full Support Troop.

The Fighting Troops, under the command of captains, were made up of two sections, each commanded by a lieutenant, with a troop sergeant to do the donkey work of controlling the men. These in turn were organized into three sub-sections of nine or ten men, each with a corporal in charge. The main weapon of the sub-section was a bren 303 inch calibre light machine-gun (LMG) which was maintained in action by a three-man 'bren group'. These were the bren-gunner, his No. 2, who fitted fresh magazines and changed the barrel when required, and the No. 3, whose job it was to keep the No. 2 supplied with ammunition, if need be by collecting clips of cartridges from the riflemen and re-filling empty magazines. The remainder of the sub-section were arranged into two 'rifle groups' each of three men, and there were also two men who handled a two-inch mortar. This arrangement was flexible, and on occasion, as was the case in the Sicily operation, a number of riflemen could be issued with tommy-guns (Thompson sub-machine-guns – TSMGs) instead of rifles. Each troop also had one man designated as a sniper, whose telescopic sights were the envy of us all.

Q Troop's objective was a group of buildings reported to be occupied by about thirty or more Italian troops. The main building of the group, standing furthest from the sea, was believed by Intelligence to be a barracks, and this was christened, 'Q House'. Other smaller buildings grouped around it were taken to be mess rooms and stores. There were also three small isolated buildings, strung out in echelon formation from the main group in the general direction of the coast; their purpose was obscure but they were assumed to be some sort of guardhouses.

After crossing the beach and scaling the cliffs, Q Troop was to assemble beside a small building near the cliff top, which would have previously been cleared by A Troop. Then we were to move off to our right, along a rough track, skirting the edge of a salt lake called Pantano Bruno (completely dried up in summer) before swinging inland to approach our objective from the rear. The route from the beach to Q House was studied on large-scale maps which were brought up to date day by day as intelligence reports reached the ship from aerial reconnaissance sorties flown by the RAF. Captain Stott, who was something of a sculptor (there had been a 'reclining figure' on his desk in the Troop office at Troon), constructed a model of the buildings, and every detail of the attack was planned with meticulous care.

The assault would be directed first at Q House, with a view to catching the enemy in their beds; then we would clear the adjacent buildings, leaving the three small 'guardhouses' to be dealt with last of all. Bren-gun positions were worked out to obtain a clear field of fire over an open space between the buildings, which had been designated 'the killing area', to which it was proposed to drive any Italians who managed to evade the first assault on the barrack block. Consideration was also given to the likely materials of construction of the various buildings, as it would be distinctly unhealthy for anyone crouching behind a light timber shed if automatic fire was being sprayed in through the front door. Having achieved this primary objective, Q Troop's subsequent moves would be dictated by the turn of events, but if Y Troop was having any trouble with their task, the gun-emplacement on the headland, we were to give them a hand.

In addition to studying the plans for the military operation, we also learned a little about the country to be invaded, from a small booklet issued to the Canadians. It gave brief notes on the geography and history of Italy, a few 'dos' and 'don'ts' of good behaviour and a list of 'words and phrases you are likely to need'. These were of the usual tourist variety, ordering meals and complaining about short change, but we also had a typewritten sheet of more warlike phrases, which we tried to learn parrot-fashion, such as, 'Where are the Germans?', 'Hands up!'. 'Carry this man!' and, our favourite, 'Be quiet or you'll be shot.' One that didn't appear particularly appropriate in the circumstances was, 'Don't be afraid – we are friends!'

Living-space for the troops on the *Durban Castle* was extremely restricted. At mealtimes there was barely enough elbow-room to manipulate the food from plate to mouth, and the mess tables were so close together that there was a continual 'scrubbling' of vertebrae with the chaps on the next mess. Once seated, it was impossible, short of walking along the table, to leave your place until the meal was finished, and everyone shuffled along the wooden form to freedom.

The portholes were permanently closed and sealed with steel covers on the inboard side, to avoid any infringement of total black-out during the hours of darkness. There was a system of metal trunking designed to convey fresh air down to the depths of the ship, but this was woefully inadequate for the numbers of men on board, so that, even in British waters, conditions on the mess decks were exceedingly hot and sticky. In spite of our wearing an absolute minimum of clothing, all sweat glands worked overtime. At mealtimes, the oozings from the forehead would trickle down the nose to fall with musical plops into your plate of what more often than not was a meat and vegetable concoction which went under the name 'brown stew'.

The official 'order' for sleeping was 'fully dressed, less boots', in case of submarine attack, but in the sweltering conditions that prevailed below decks, this was rarely adhered to. On a number of occasions, during the hours of darkness, we felt the ominous hammer-blows of exploding depth-charges reverberate through the ship's hull and suffered the mental anguish of considering whether to get dressed in a hurry or risk going into the sea wearing only vest and pants. Every flat surface within the mess deck had to double up as a bed. The most sought-after places were on or under the mess table and on the mess seating. These were strictly private to those who managed to appropriate them, were safe from wandering feet, and even the atmosphere there wasn't quite so fuggy as in the 'hammock belt' above.

Some hammocks were available, but it wasn't unusual to find that, in the general mêlée of bedding down, and up, for the night, those already occupied had been slung in such haphazard confusion that, although there were many hooks not in use, no two were suitably placed to allow another hammock to be slung. Then, apart from the problems of slinging, many men were deterred from using them by the extra hassle involved in having to 'lash up and stow' in order to clear the mess deck in the morning. The great majority were content to adopt the simpler alternative of just curling up on any vacant area of deckspace.

Those first to turn in would settle down in the more secluded corners where they would have a good chance of remaining undisturbed throughout the night. Then the tide of recumbent forms would spread progressively outwards until the late arrivals, drifting away from card schools and crap games in the early hours, had no option but to stretch out in the gangways and other circulation areas. Dim lights burned throughout the night as, with hundreds of men on every mess deck, there was always someone going somewhere – or trying to locate where he had been before he went. Long before official reveille – as early as 0400 – dozens of men had abandoned any further attempts at sleeping and were taking advantage of the uncrowded 'ablutions' to wash, shave or shower.

Conditions below decks dictated that as much time as possible was spent in the open air, but overcrowding was an even greater problem on the upper decks. This was particularly acute during the mornings, when mess decks were Out of Bounds, while the Officer Commanding Troops made his rounds. Until his tour of the ship was over (and it could last until noon), there was nothing to do but stand around, unless you were lucky enough to have a capstan or winch housing to sit on, and talk – or be talked to by your officers.

It was only in the afternoons that the overwhelming demand on deck space in the open air eased sufficiently to permit any sort of group activity, but even this had to be on a strict rota basis, to cater for all the military formations on board. It was then that we received our daily dose of physical jerks under our lean, lanky and much-tattooed PT instructor, Sergeant Crookes. There were also a few inter-unit boxing matches and tugs-of-war but it was a problem to clear enough deck area to allow them to take place with a reasonable amount of space for spectators.

Below decks there wasn't a great deal to do either, after the daily session of studying maps and photographs in the operations room. An infrequent quiz, then it was reading, writing letters, playing cards and stripping the bren. The bren light machine-gun (its name came from Brno, the Czechoslovakian town where it originated, and Enfield the North London suburb where it was subsequently manufactured) supplied the bulk of the firepower of an infantry section, and every man was trained in its use. It was an air-cooled weapon, and prolonged firing necessitated the fitting of a fresh barrel after every ten magazines, to avoid damage through overheating. Removal of the barrel was the first of a whole sequence of operations, requiring no more than deft fingers, which could reduce the weapon to its constituent parts, right down to the smallest spring of the 'trigger group'. With practice it could all be done blindfolded, and it wasn't at all unusual to see two or three marines with stocking caps over their eyes, sitting with brens in front of them, awaiting the word 'GO!' Then the contest was to see who could strip the gun down to the smallest spring and reassemble everything again in the shortest possible time.

In this restricted way life passed pleasantly enough but, as we had to stand in line for every necessity, the simple process of living was very time-consuming. Yet time didn't seem to hang too heavily on our hands for, as so often seems to be the case, when there is little to do, there hardly seems time to do anything. The weather continued fine, growing warmer day by day as our convoy steamed unhurriedly towards the Mediterranean.

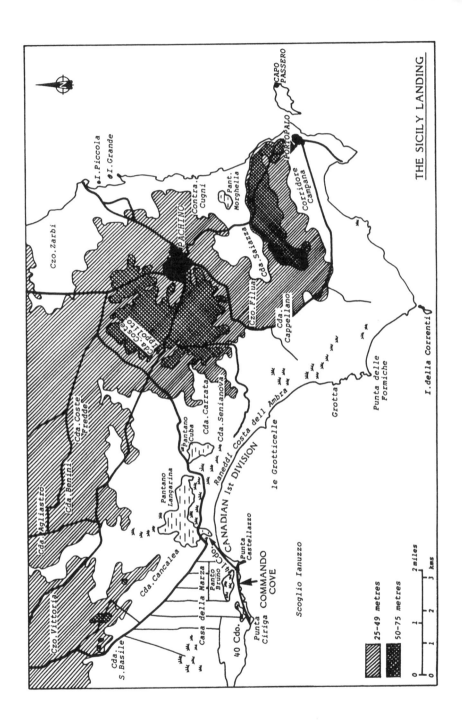

THE SICILY LANDING

3 Nearing Our Goal

Passage through the Straits of Gibraltar was effected during the early hours of 6 July, eight days out from Gourock. There were only a few of us lining the ship's rails to watch the black silhouettes of the other vessels gliding effortlessly over the calm sea, polished to a silvery grey by the light of the moon, and to gaze at the black, indistinct but still unmistakable hump of 'The Rock' as it slipped slowly astern.

Royal Marines have had a proprietary interest in Gibraltar ever since their predecessors took possession of it for the Crown in 1704 and subsequently defended it against the armies of France and Spain. The word 'Gibraltar' forms part of the Corps crest, and even we, hostilities-only marines (HOs) were sufficiently well versed in Corps history to know all this – and had been imbued with enough pride in 'our' battle honours to prompt us to make the effort of giving up some sleep just to see where it had all started. Some few of the unit were continuous-service marines (CSs) – men who had signed up for twelve years with the colours, and there was some good-humoured banter between the two varieties. The only way of telling them apart was by their regimental numbers, and any disgruntled man heard muttering, 'Roll on, my twelve' (years) could very well have signed up only 'for the duration of the present emergency', although at that stage of the war no one could be certain which term of service would be the longer.

Once we were in the Mediterranean, our battledress uniform (BDs) was returned to stores and we donned khaki service dress (KSDs). There was some curiosity and a little trepidation about the likely reception of such a convoy in what Mussolini (aping the ancient Romans) had vaingloriously called 'Mare Nostrum' ('Our Sea'). Memories of the concentrated aerial attacks on the Malta convoys of the previous year were still fresh in our minds – but it remained 'our' sea, rather than the Italians', with everything continuing to be idyllically peaceful. The sun blazed hotly from a cloudless blue sky, and our widely spaced ships moved majestically onwards, slicing bows scarcely disturbing the deeper blue of a placid sea. For much of the first two days we were in sight of the North African coast, and the snow-covered peaks of the Atlas Mountains stood out sharp and silvery in the clear, sparkling air. How many enemy agents, we wondered, were up in those hills with binoculars, noting down the number and types of ship steaming eastwards.

An unexpected feature of our voyage to war now manifested itself in the ever-increasing number of bald heads to be seen around the ship. With the weather growing daily warmer and the prospect of more heat to come, there was a craze for the ultimate in short haircuts, and a surprising variety of craniums was revealed. The most remarkable was probably that of one of our Scotsmen, Evan Bath, as there was hardly a square inch of his pate that didn't bear some scar – from bottle, brickbat or razor, all said to be mementos of gang-fights in the streets of his native Glasgow. Matt Walsh, our sub-section corporal, wasn't slow to exploit the humorous possibilities it presented. Tucking Evan's head under his left arm and using the intersecting lines of puckered flesh as a map, he would trace out the route of an imaginary military operation. The briefing would last for just as long as Evan condescended to play along – when he would terminate proceedings with an elbow jab into Matt's solar plexus.

The warmth of the sun was very tempting, but sunbathing was strictly forbidden. We were warned that the inability to wear webbing equipment as a result of sunburn would be classed as a 'self-inflicted wound', and the slightest suspicion that someone was removing his bush shirt would immediately bring forth the command,

'Get covered up there!'. But the forward movement of the ship created a cooling breeze, and it was pleasant to lie on a warm, snoozy deck (when you were able to locate a vacant spot) – 'Guests of a grateful Government', as the wags put it.

Half-dozing in the warmth of the sun, the mind's eye would take you back to the maps, models and photographs in the operations room – and off you would go once again on the route you had studied so many times already ... down the ramp, across the beach, up the cliffs, over the coastal road to that small building – hopefully cleared by A Troop, move off half-right, around Pantano Bruno, then turn inland to pass Q House on your right, circle around to the rear, bren group – there, rifle groups forward, troop sergeant and tommy-gunner to the door ... We had carried out this sort of exercise many times before but now, lying on the pulsing deck of a troopship under the hot Mediterranean sun, it had at last sunk into our minds that this time it would be the real thing.

The invasion of Sicily had been set for the early hours of Saturday 10 July, so final preparations were reaching their climax on the Wednesday and Thursday. Each man was issued with his personal rations for the first forty-eight hours ashore – corned beef, cheese, butter, jam, hardtack biscuits and the inevitable 'compo' tea (a mixture of tea, sugar and dried milk). The diet was as expected but the extra weight of these canned foods on top of our already considerable burdens occasioned many lurid comments.

Water-bottles were filled and a pinch of salt was added to compensate for that which we would soon be sweating out of our bodies. Each man also received a bottle of sterilizing tablets, to be used before drinking the local water, together with a similar bottle of another type of tablet designed to take away the taste of the first ones! To enable us to boil water, we were also issued with an individual 'Tommy cooker' (little more than a tin can with airholes) and a supply of fuel pellets. At that stage of the war it was generally believed that the Germans referred to Sherman tanks as 'Tommy cookers' – allegedly because of their tendency, when hit, to burst into flames (or 'brew up' as it was generally called), with the implied dire effects upon their crews – but it seems doubtful whether such a play on words could be equally effective in both languages.

Ammunition was issued on the Thursday. Magazines for the brens and tommy-guns were filled, each round first being given a smear of grease around the firing-cap, which it was hoped would ensure that they would still function properly should we have a wet landing. In addition to his own personal weapons and ammunition, each man carried three hand-grenades – two 36s (the 'Mill's bomb', high-explosive, fragmentation type) and one 68 (which generated smoke for screening purposes). Each rifleman also carried an extra bandolier of fifty rounds of 303 cartridges, plus two full magazines for the bren. As a tommy-gunner on this occasion, I was considered to be sufficiently heavily laden with my own ten (twenty-round) magazines. There was a near calamity on a crowded upper deck when grenades were being primed when someone inadvertently pulled out the pin after inserting the fuse. Only the split second reaction of a sergeant got it over the side before exploding.

By this time it was clear that we would be going ashore laden like pack animals, and when a belated intelligence report advised of the possibility of 'false beaches' (submerged sandbanks at some distance from the shore), there arose the vision of having to swim for it. This alerted the more ruthless types to the fact that one inflatable lifebelt might not be sufficient to support them with all their impedimenta, and there developed a spate of mysteriously disappearing 'Mae Wests'. For the first time on the voyage it was not unusual to see men wearing them day and night.

We were also issued with a few items of specifically 'commando' equipment (designed to help us make good our escape in the event of capture), which had to be secreted about our persons. These included maps printed on silk, miniature files and a variety of ingenious compasses which could be sewn into the seams of your uniform. The final touch was a pay parade at which we each received the equivalent of 10 shillings pay (at that time, in Britain, a shilling would purchase twenty cigarettes) in 'Invasion money', Allied Military Government Lire, for use after the fighting was over. Dress for the landing was to be 'fighting order and long KSDs'. Khaki service dress was issued with one pair of shorts to wear by day and one pair of long trousers for night-time, when it was important to protect as much skin as possible from the malaria-inducing bite of the female mosquito. In 'fighting order' the small pack, which was fitted to the belt in marching order, was rearranged onto the back webbing straps of the equipment. Our big packs were filled with such gear (change of clothing, spare boots, drinking mugs, etc) and personal belongings (letters, photographs and writing materials) as was to follow us ashore when things had quietened down.

As a last thorn in the flesh, on that Thursday morning, barely forty hours before 'H-hour', a destroyer came alongside with the latest aerial photographs of Commando Cove, which appeared to show that barbed wire had recently been laid in the sea close to the beach. It was much too late to take any measures to counter-act such a possibility, so it was just another matter on which we would have to 'wait and see'.

During the afternoon, the Mediterranean, which had previously been so calm and serene, started to cut up rough. By evening, high seas were running and gale-force winds were blowing the tops off the waves. Next morning, weather conditions were little changed but we could now see that our convoy had been joined by score upon score of other ships – the whole sea, for as far as the eye could see, was covered with vessels of every imaginable size and type. It seemed impossible that the Italians or Germans or whoever could be unaware of our presence. The *Durban Castle* was rolling and pitching so much that the majority of the troops on board were now deep in the miseries of sea-sickness. For those with less susceptible stomachs, this was an unexpected bonus, as it became possible to move around the upper decks with much greater freedom.

By the afternoon of Friday, the wind and sea had abated

considerably but it still seemed extremely doubtful whether a landing would be possible that night. Nevertheless, we checked again that our closest friends still had the note of our home addresses, 'just in case', and re-affirmed our own promises to write to their wives or parents 'should anything happen'. We never used the phrase 'getting killed'.

In the afternoon the Padre held a special communion service and, unlike the usual church parades, attendance was entirely voluntary. Nevertheless, it was exceptionally well attended as many who would normally go to great lengths to avoid such occasions considered that it might not be a bad idea to attend this particular one. I am sure that most felt they derived some sort of benefit from going.

Afterwards we were advised to try to get some sleep just in case the landing should prove possible, but I suspect that few succeeded, even though, thanks to sea-sickness, there was a choice of sheltered spots on the upper decks where you could lie down and close your eyes. My mind, like the ship, just could not keep still and continued to rehearse the part we were to play in the coming invasion and to speculate on the possibility of a postponement. At 1700 hours the *Hilary*, Admiral Vian's headquarter ship, lowered a black ball to synchronize all timepieces throughout the convoy – but this didn't tell us whether or not the invasion would in fact go ahead.

The day dragged along until at about nine o'clock in the evening, we sat down for what would be our last meal on board – if the landing was to take place. The fact that for some it could very well be their last meal on earth was pushed to the back of the mind. When the cooks of the mess returned with the trays of food, it was found to be the all-too-familiar concoction of semi-liquid meat and vegetables. A Cockney voiced the feelings of us all. 'Blimey!' he ejaculated. 'Brahn stoo – agine! Woo'n't yer think they'd've given us somefin' decent *this* time??' Brown stew or not, there wasn't much left to return to the galley, so most appetites had returned to normal. After the meal there was another check of weapons, ammunition and equipment before lying down, fully rigged, to await the order – to go or not to go.

I had crawled under the mess table and must have fallen asleep, as the next thing I knew the gravelly voice of Sergeant Shepherd was bawling, 'All right, Q Troop – on your feet!' It must be on! I squirmed out into the dim glow of the blue operational lights and lit a cigarette before starting to collect my paraphernalia. All around, half-awake figures were swaying with the motion of the ship as they adjusted arms and equipment, many racked with uncontrollable bouts of coughing after that first long drag on a cigarette.

With all our gear in place, Mae West lifebelt on top of everything, and weapons slung over shoulders, we lined up in front of a steaming bucketful of cocoa for a farewell drink. The lingering hopes of a generous tot of Navy rum before going ashore, which some had nurtured right to the last, were finally dissipated. The whole trip had been 'dry' – and now we knew that it was to stay that way to the end: it was cocoa or nothing.

With the drink finished and the bucket returned to the galley, we stood around awaiting the next order, but minute followed minute and nothing happened. One by one we began to unsling weapons and sit down again – on the seats, the mess table, the deck, anywhere. What the heck, we wondered, is happening now? Faces, indistinct and eerie in the blue dimness of the operational lights, were being highlighted at ever shorter intervals by the warm glow of deeply inhaled cigarettes. The ship continued to roll and pitch, and there were still some mutterings of, 'It's too bloody rough.' But for most of us the feeling was, 'For Christ's sake, let's get the fricking thing over and done with.'

The loudspeakers clicked into life, and ears pricked up expectantly. It was about one o'clock in the morning by this time. 'First wave, stand by. First wave, stand by ...' So it's on, in spite of the weather! It was some relief to know that we wouldn't have to unwind again, and a buzz of excited banter filled the mess deck. 'Winston bloody Churchill should be here,' somebody wisecracked, 'get some of that fricking fat off him.' There was a ripple of laughter as we re-slung our weapons and 'got fell in', taking up the well-drilled positions for moving up to the landing-craft. Last cigarettes were lit from the stubs of the old before stowing the packet and matches inside steel helmets, where they would have the best chance of a dry landing.

The Tannoy clicked again. 'Serial 352 – muster abreast your craft. Serial 352 – muster abreast your craft'. That's us! 'All right,' barked Sergeant Shepherd. 'Out pipes – get moving!' Not for the first time did we wonder why NCOs invariably prefaced their commands with, 'All right', when more often than not it was anything but all right. One last drag before grinding half-smoked cigarettes underfoot and tramping off in single file along the mess deck. Then we were climbing the companionways, moving up towards our boat deck.

Here and there we passed huddles of Canadians, in their shirtsleeves, waiting to wish us well. They still had a few more hours on board, as it was our job to make sure that there were no guns firing on them from the Punta Castellazzo as they were landing. 'Good luck, lads!' they called out. 'Give 'em Hell!' – as well as other, more coarsely phrased advice. Even when we had stepped from the warmth of the ship's interior onto the open deck and felt the cool night air on our faces, there were still groups of Canadians bunched together in the shadows to see us on our way.

There was no moon – which was to our liking – but the sky was clear, and under a canopy of countless stars there was light enough to see our way along the deck and take up position beside the LCAs. We looked hard in the direction of the Sicilian coast some eight miles away but it was completely lost in the darkness. Awaiting the order to climb into the craft, we studied the sea far below. It was much blacker than the sky but we could easily make out the curling white splashes of the waves as they slapped against the ship's side – it didn't look at all inviting.

Notwithstanding the distance from the shore, the occasion seemed to demand that the order to board landing-craft be given in a subdued voice, and it was. We stepped from the rolling but comparatively stable deck of the *Durban Castle* into the swinging assault craft which was now dangling freely from its davits. Bill Smith, the bren-gunner for our craft, moved forward to his little cubbyhole in the bows, where he could, if required, provide some kind of covering fire when the craft was moving in for touchdown. From his right hand dangled 'Betsy', as he jovially called his gun. We never enquired just why he had chosen that particular name for his bren, but it may have been that he liked Davy Crockett, who always referred to his rifle as 'Old Betsy' – Bill's bren was obviously a much younger lady.

The rest of us, numbering twenty-five or twenty-six men, settled down into uncomfortable squatting positions on the bottom of the craft, two files under the narrow decking along the sides and the third along the open centre line. The matelot at the winch started to lower away, and we began the long descent to the Mediterranean.

A deep Canadian voice followed us down the ship's side: 'Leave some of the bastards for us ...'

4 The Invasion of Sicily

The landing-craft struck the water with a smack that jolted the steel helmets over our eyes. A sailor released the lowering-tackle, and as the engines blurrrrrped into life, we pulled away from the ship's side. At close quarters we found the sea to be even more disturbed than it had appeared from the lofty boat deck of the *Durban Castle*. Our thirty-foot craft, slapped and buffeted by the rolling waves, was tossed about like a matchbox in a bathtub. Squatting low in the darkness of the bottom of the boat, our range of vision was restricted to the dim forms of our nearest neighbours: we could see nothing of what was happening outside. As the LCA bucked, rolled and crashed against the seas, it wasn't long before most of the chaps were being violently sick. Harold Colloff, slumped next to me, sounded as though he wouldn't have cared in the slightest if the bottom of the boat were to open up and drop him into the sea. All around, the interior of the craft was becoming more and more polluted with second-hand brown stew and cocoa.

There was always a short period of hanging about after leaving the ship, while the LCAs circled around, waiting until the whole 'wave' had unhooked and formed up ready for the approach run to the shore. This time we realized that the delay was much longer than usual. No reason was given, so we just assumed that the roughness of the sea was making things that much more difficult. Eventually we felt the engine surge to full power and, as the landing-craft bludgeoned its way through the heavy seas, every impact of its blunt bows sent a cascade of spray over the crouching marines. In our confined positions, leg muscles were already cramped and painful and shoulders ached under the dead load of weapons and equipment. The stench of vomit and the continuing sound of retching added their quota to the general discomfort.

We had a long way to go, so it was a great relief to be given permission to stand up, stretch throbbing limbs and flush out our lungs with gulps of fresh air. Grasping the edges of the narrow decking to maintain balance, we revelled in the cool water of the Mediterranean splashing wetly into our faces and trickling a clean salty taste into the corners of our mouths. Looking around for the *Durban Castle*, we were surprised to see that she, along with the entire task force, had already been swallowed up by the night. We were alone – our two lines of landing-craft bouncing madly through the waves had the whole sea to themselves. The LCAs were running parallel to the low, dark silhouette that was Sicily, lying a few miles away to starboard. We, No. 7 section of Q Troop, were in the column nearest to the shore. To port, the other craft of the first wave were no more than indistinct black blotches which at times were completely obliterated by showers of white spray as they bucked and splashed their way over the troubled sea. It was difficult to appreciate that those black shapes were small steel boxes just like the one we were in and that each one carried a load of armed men on their way to invade enemy territory.

Then the indistinct smear of land to our right was no longer entirely black. White fingers of searchlights began to wheel back and forth across the night sky. This was comforting, as the RAF should now be attacking Pachino. Even above the continuous roar of the landing-craft's engines we could make out the dull drone of aircraft passing overhead – but no sight or sound of exploding bombs reached us. Perhaps the aeroplanes weren't bombers after all but engaged in carrying paratroopers to their dropping-zone further up the coast. Our sea-sick comrades were still retching on empty stomachs, but all the groans and grurrrrps were magically stilled by the unmistakable 'boooommm' of a medium-heavy gun reverberating across the water. Anti-aircraft or coast defence? We held our breath, ears cocked, counting the seconds for the tell-tale scream of an approaching shell – but nothing. Whoever had fired must have had aimed elsewhere. But why only one round? There was no point in trying to guess. At least the anti-sea-sickness effect was lasting. Everyone could turn their full attention to the job in hand.

The inshore waters were much calmer, and flashes of phosphorescence could now be seen dancing about the bows of the other craft. The coastline had resolved itself into a distinct black shape, less than a mile away, when the landing-craft turned to starboard and arranged themselves into line-abreast formation for the final run-in to the beach. We received the order 'Get down!', and sank back into the gloom below the gunwhales, crouching low on left knees, right legs bent and ready for the push forward. I adjusted the tommy-gun sling on my shoulder, firmly clutching the pistol grip with my right hand. My left hand gripped the neck of a sandbag, partially filled with clips of 303 cartridges, which I was required to drop on the beach as a contribution to the ammunition reserve. Not long now! The engines were throttled back – the bullet-proof steel doors in the bows creaked open. Muscles tensed ready to spring forward, all eyes firmly fixed on the back of the head of the man in front.

The naval officer in charge of the craft began quietly to call out the distance to the shore: '500 yards ... 400 ... 300.' The only sounds were the low hum of the engines and a gentle slapping of the sea against the bows as we nosed slowly in towards the beach. '200 ... 100.' Abruptly, the silence was shattered by the harsh rattle of a machine-gun. Ours or theirs? There was scarcely time to formulate the thought before we grounded with a slight judder; the ramp thumped down with a splash into the sea. No time to wonder about false beaches or wire in the water or mines in the sand. Our reaction, bred of long training, was automatic. Up sandbag and run! ... along the craft ... down the ramp and into the water. It came to just above our knees, and the going was heavy, but at least we were on a real beach for, only about thirty yards away, there stretched the flat sand of Commando Cove.

The machine-gun was chattering away continuously but nothing was coming in my direction. Shadowy figures splashed through the water beside me, their identities indistinguishable in the semi-darkness. I had almost reached the beach and had just realized that the cliffs beyond the sand did not appear to be nearly as high or as steep as expected when I tripped and fell full length into a few inches of water. Almost before I knew what had happened I was up again, splashing on across the foreshore, then stumbling through the deep, soft sand of the beach. Thankfully dropping the bag of cartridges, I saw with some relief that the 'cliffs' were no more than high sand dunes, and scrambled up to the top, went forward a few yards to what should have been our assembly point and flopped to the ground sweating and panting. My first concern was for my weapon, so I whipped off the magazine lest it had collected some sand during its brief immersion, pushed it in a pocket of my bush shirt and fitted a fresh one from an ammunition pouch. As I did so, my brain unconsciously formulated the oft-repeated admonition of our small-arms instructors: '... and don't forget to re-fasten the pouch ...' We couldn't afford to lose valuable ammunition. I snapped it shut.

Only then did I begin to wonder what had happened to the rest of the section. A second machine-gun had now joined the first, and this time I recognized the rather sloppy, loose kind of rattle from the floating piston of the Italian breda. From a short distance to my right, low moans of pain told that A Troop was suffering casualties. I had also realized that there was no building in the immediate vicinity, nor had I crossed the anticipated coastal track. Feeling alone and out of things, I slithered back down to the beach to find the others of the section, all rather wet and out of breath, just waiting for me to show up. We moved back over the crest of the dunes, and by this time other groups of men were assembling to both sides of us. We could hear Lieutenant Lloyd, No. 8 section commander, conferring with the second-in-command. It filtered down to us that Captain Stott, with the other half of Q Troop had gone missing. No one appeared to know the reason but it was quickly decided that we should carry on without them.

Commands were whispered back. 'A' Troop was to silence the machine-gun to our right while Q, such as it was, would do a left flanking movement to skirt around the opposition, then carry on with the Troop task. We moved forward, running bent double towards the top of another rise in the ground. More shadowy figures, indistinct and unrecognizable, were crouching low just below the skyline ahead of us. A stream of bullets swept over the brow of the hill, causing some commotion up front. A sick-berth attendant slithered back down the line of climbing men enquiring urgently, 'Are you an officer? One of the chaps needs morphia.' Ampules were carried only by commissioned officers, so we directed him back to where we had last encountered the other Troop officer, Lieutenant Haydon. The section now veered off to the left, bent low to stay below the line of fire. We travelled rapidly and soon left the protection of the hillside to move across a stretch of open country where the going was once again, soft sand. By now the webbing straps of our equipment were cutting painfully into shoulders through the thin khaki drill of our bush shirts. In my nostrils there was already building up a pungent, not unpleasant but haunting smell, which must have been a combination of sea, sand, cactus, vines and goodness knows what else that, for years afterwards, my brain could faithfully conjure up as the odour of Sicily.

With the combined efforts of moving fast, bending low and preventing our weapons from trailing in the soft earth, we were sweating like pigs. It was a welcome respite therefore when Lieutenant Lloyd came to an abrupt halt and we heard his stage-whisper command, 'Corporal Taylor – cut those wires!' In the half light we could just discern a rather stumpy pole carrying what must have been a few telephone wires and heard Buck Taylor's panting response, 'Who, sir? *Me*, sir??' As I crouched low to the ground, sucking in lungfuls of night air and trying to calm a madly thumping heart, I couldn't help but grin into the darkness. Lloydie had inadvertently chosen the only man of the Troop to have fallen from a tree during rope-climbing exercises at Achnacarry, when he had suffered a dislocated shoulder. But Buck's response must have been involuntary rather than protesting. He shinned up the pole, and as soon as we heard the 'snip, snip, snip' of the wire-cutters, the section moved on. From the middle distance to our right we heard the dull thump of a bursting grenade followed by a fusillade of rifle shots and a few yells of triumph. 'A' Troop had silenced their machine-gun.

We swung back on course for Q House, moving quickly over an open area covered with low, bushy plants. The going was still soft and in the poor light we tripped and stumbled continually. A sudden pause up front brought our single file to a dead stop. We sank down on one knee, weapons at the ready. Now that we had come to close quarters with the bushes which had been tripping us, it could be seen that they were lowly grapevines. Everyone's immediate concern, however, was a string of shadowy figures, half left to our front, which was moving towards us. 'Hold your fire!' The order was whispered back down the line, but almost simultaneously the sharp crack of a rifle shot rang out from a few yards back down our column. The advancing figures sank low into the vines, and everyone awaited the next move. A quick backward glance confirmed that it had indeed been Mick Donovan, our Cockney Irishman, who had squeezed the trigger. Then we heard Lieutenant Lloyd's voice calling out the password challenge for the invasion, 'Desert Rats!' It immediately brought forth the correct response, 'Kill Italians!' We had encountered some men from another Troop, wandering a little off course, so it was with common relief that we all carried on with our respective missions.

At the far side of the field, we passed through a hedge of cactuses and found ourselves on a stony path curving gradually round to the right, in the general direction of our objective. We had followed this track for only a few minutes when there was another sudden halt. From the head of the column came the sound of a few metallic clicks and some low cursing. More clicks were followed by more curses, and these were quickly followed by the whispered call of 'Tommy-gunner!' coming down the line. I moved up to the head of the section and knelt down beside Lieutenant Haydon, who was now leading the way. It appeared that Corporal Taylor's tommy-gun couldn't be persuaded to fire, so mine was the next to be tried. The officer pointed to something low and circular just discernible in the gloom twenty or so yards ahead. 'Give it a burst, Mitchell,' he ordered. I raised the gun to my shoulder, took aim and squeezed the trigger. 'Brrrrrrrrrrp' – it worked like a charm. There were no yells nor screams but in the ensuing silence we heard the unmistakable splatter of splintered masonry falling into the still water of a Sicilian well.

The section pressed on, but now, as the custodian of the only effective tommy-gun, I stayed up front, immediately behind Lieutenant Haydon. By this time the countryside was becoming alive with the rattle of brens, the detonation of hand-grenades and the crackle of rifle fire as the Commando went about its various tasks. In addition we now had for background music a medley of 'whoomps' and 'crumps' from the bursting shells of naval guns engaging their allotted targets. Occasionally a shell would burst in our vicinity, but these must have been strays. One, fortuitously, landed immediately to our front – only about a hundred yards away and very close to Q Troop's objective. For a fraction of a second the brilliant flash of the explosion illuminated a group of white buildings which were instantly recognizable from Captain Stott's model. We didn't know if that shell had arrived with the compliments of the Royal Navy or whether it was from an enemy battery, but whoever was firing obligingly found somewhere else to drop them before we moved any closer.

Pushing on without pause, it had become apparent that our advance was being directed towards the front of the objective, instead of swinging to the left in order to attack it from the rear, as had been rehearsed in our minds so many times. Perhaps the near-miss of the artillery shell, or the fact that we were only half a Troop, had changed the plan, but no reason was given. It also became apparent that the intention was to deal with the three 'guardhouses' first, rather than leaving them to last. As we were approaching the first one, there was just sufficient light to make out the officer's signal to move into extended line. With Lieutenant Lloyd in the centre, we advanced silently, picking our way carefully through another patch of stunted vines. When within about twenty yards of the building, we received the signal 'Down!' Sergeant Shepherd came across and, with a tap on the shoulder and a curt inclination of the head, told me to get up and follow him. Together with two other marines – the 'terrible twins', Harry Weiss and Bill Marshall – and Lieutenant Haydon, we sprinted towards the door and positioned ourselves ready to make an entry.

Harry and Bill ranged themselves on either side of the doorway, rifles cocked, bayonets fixed, all ready to charge in. The officer and sergeant were also against the wall with pistols in their hands. I had positioned myself, in accordance with the appropriate paragraph of the training manual, directly in front of the door and about two yards away, down on one knee, tommy-gun all set to fire, finger on the trigger. Shep waved his gun, signalling 'Here goes!', fired two rounds into the lock and crashed the door open with his foot. As he stepped to one side, I was in the doorway, my spluttering gun spraying bullets into the black interior.

Hardly had I stepped back to allow the riflemen to take over than the terrified screams of two or three children rang out from the darkness. 'Good God! You've killed some kids!' The thought had barely formed itself in my brain before everything became completely silent once more. Was it some kind of a trap? Moving cautiously inside, weapons at the ready, we found a whole family of father, mother and three or more children all cowering in one large bed. Fortunately, for my sake as well as theirs, it was against the front wall, behind the door we had just forced open. All were scared out of their wits but, mercifully, completely unharmed. My heart started beating again – thank God, we hadn't used a grenade! After making sure that they would just stay where they were, we checked the other two small houses – and found that they too were no more than the one-roomed homes of Sicilian peasants.

At this point the operation – so far as I was concerned – became somewhat confused. There were consultations in the dim light of approaching dawn, and Lieutenant Lloyd departed with the remnants of his section on some mission or other. Lieutenant Haydon too went missing for a short while; then he returned with an Italian prisoner. This soldier, we were told, was home on leave and had been only too happy to give himself up. But how he came to be wandering around in full uniform in the early hours of the morning was something of a puzzle. Nor did I ever understand why there was nobody around but me when Lieutenant Haydon decided to push on to Q House and told me to accompany him. He moved off up a narrow footpath running between high hedges, towards the main buildings of the Troop objective. In his right hand he brandished his revolver; with his left he had a firm grip on the Italian prisoner just above the right elbow. 'So he's coming too!' I thought. We halted at a line of man-sized cactuses and peered across the dozen or so yards of bare ground separating us from a line of buildings. Directly ahead and immediately recognizable stood the building that was to have been the task of my sub-section. Close by to our right stood the long white 'barracks' building which was the Troop's primary objective. The officer waved his gun in the direction of the nearest building and whispered, 'Go on, Mitchell, clear that building. I'll cover you with my pistol.'

A vision of the carefully rehearsed attack, with the bren group supporting two assault groups of riflemen, flashed through my mind before I sprinted across the open ground to flatten myself against the wall of the building, immediately to the left of a large open doorway. The only noise to be heard was the mad thumping of my heart. I poked the muzzle of the tommy-gun around the doorpost and squeezed the trigger. After only three or four rounds the magazine ran out – black mark, Mitchell. I pulled back from the doorway to fit a fresh one. But there had been absolutely no reaction to my shooting – everything remained completely calm and peaceful; so I decided not to fire again. Instead, I advanced circumspectly through the doorway. Apart from two massive casks, presumably for the storage of *vino* and quite possibly punctured as a result of my little effort, plus a miscellaneous collection of farm implements, the place was empty. 'OK, sir,' I called back. 'Not a sausage!'

The rest of the sub-section now emerged magically from the semi-darkness, and we all moved towards Q House. There was little doubt that what British Intelligence had taken to be a military establishment was no more than a group of farm buildings and cottages. This was soon made abundantly clear when a bevy of some seven or eight extremely vociferous Sicilian ladies debouched from 'the barracks'. The Italian words we had been at pains to learn had now to be put to the test. Our repeated '*Tah-chee-tay!* *Tah-chee-tay!*' (*Tacite!* 'Quiet!') eventually calmed things down, so I decided to carry the experiment a little further with, '*Non abbiate paura!*' ('Don't be afraid!') and followed this up with the phrase which had seemed so unlikely ever to be of use, '*Noi siamo amici!*' ('We are friends!') This proved to be an immediate success. The ladies took up the cry of '*amici*' *en masse* until the farmyard echoed to '*Ahmeechee!*', '*Ahmeechee!*', *Ahmeechee!*' over and over again. But we couldn't afford to hang around chatting, being more concerned about quiet enemies than noisy friends, so we bundled them indoors with a combination of English, Italian and the waving of guns, to make it clear that they should get back inside, stay there and shut up.

By this time – it must have been something after 4 a.m. – the sky had lightened perceptibly with the approach of dawn. We moved off in single file at a quick march. Being much more able to distinguish our surroundings, we soon recognized the Italian strongpoint of Casa della Marza (which commanded the only exit from the Canadian beach) standing some six or seven hundred yards away and directly ahead of us. This we knew was P Troop's objective. We were also aware that Q Troop's follow-up task was to support A at the gun-emplacement, which meant that we should have been swinging away to the right of the Casa, instead of being led straight towards it. This further change of plan made us more bewildered. Our advance was soon brought to a halt by a barrier of barbed wire, clearly the perimeter of the Italian position, all in accordance with the briefing. Bullets were now zipping over our heads, a clear indication that in this instance Intelligence had been right: the Casa *was* a strongpoint and clearly still manned.

We had flopped to the ground beneath a few straggling almond trees as bullets slashed through the branches, slicing off leaves which fluttered down upon our heads. Sergeant Cole reported having detected the area of the Casa from which the firing was coming. Lieutenant Haydon sent a man crawling forward to cut the wire, then called back for the bren-gunner. Up doubled Bill, bent very low, with Betsy skimming the ground. He flopped down near us and was directed to open fire at a particular window of the building. Bill lined up his sights, released the safety catch and squeezed the trigger. Nothing! Automatically he carried out the 'First IA' (First Immediate Action – what to do if the gun doesn't fire): press (the trigger), pull back (the cocking handle) and press again. Still nothing! Rapidly he fitted a fresh magazine and went through the whole procedure once more – but got absolutely no response from Betsy. 'Here, let me have a go!' growled Sergeant Shepherd, grabbing the gun. But despite repeating all of Bill's actions – and everything being fully in accordance with laid-down procedure, the bren-gun just refused to function.

While this was going on, bullets were still whizzing about near us, and on one occasion I felt a spurt of soil on my left hand from a particularly close one. I was just lying there doing what all good soldiers do when they have no direct orders to carry out – keeping my head down. This must have been to such good effect that Lieutenant Haydon, only a yard or two away, could see no more than my steel helmet. There was no doubt in my mind as to whom he was referring when I heard him mutter rather testily to the sergeant. 'Who's that man?' I raised my head and confirmed my identity by saying, 'Mitchell, sir!' before resuming a close contemplation of Mother Earth.

Heavy small-arms fire now started coming over from our left rear. Clearly P Troop were moving in to attack *their* objective. In our exposed position we were ideally situated to be caught in a cross-fire from both sides – and most of us knew darn well that we shouldn't have been there at all. Happily, almost at that very instant we heard, above the noise of the firing, the voice of Lieutenant Lloyd bawling to Haydon, 'Peter! Bring your section over here, QUICK!' His voice had come from behind a low bank of earth, lined with the already familiar cactuses, some thirty or forty yards away to our right. We received the order to 'stand by to move' and, when there was a lull in the firing, the one word, 'NOW!' As a man we jumped to our feet, streaked across the intervening ground and dived through the cactus hedge. Rolling down the bank on the other side, we found ourselves on a wide, stony track, with a distant view of the sea.

5 *On the Left Flank of the Canadians*

As we lay against the bank side, we heard the small-arms fire from the direction of the Casa della Marza rise to a brief crescendo, then peter out altogether. The Casa had been the last of the Commando's tasks, so all objectives had now been achieved. A green Very light arched its way into the rapidly brightening sky to pass the one-word signal 'Success!' to the rest of the Commando Brigade and to all those waiting on the ships at sea. The way was now clear for the Canadians to start coming ashore.

We of Q Troop had been arranged into a defensive position along the line of dried-up ditch to await further orders. For the first time since leaving the mess deck of the *Durban Castle* to board the landing-craft some four or five hours earlier – which already seemed aeons ago and in a completely different existence, we could talk freely and actually see the people to whom we were speaking. Appealing looks and gestures towards the Troop sergeant brought permission to 'carry on smoking', and there was a flurry of striking matches and billowing cigarette smoke.

In the near-holiday atmosphere which quickly developed, we marvelled at finding ourselves safely ashore on enemy territory with few casualties – and none within my immediate circle of friends. Later I learned that Bill Marshall had had a close shave in the first burst of machine-gun fire on landing, when a bullet had struck his pack as he flopped to the ground. This had convinced him that he had been wounded – and Harry Weiss was inclined to think the same when he felt a sticky mess on Bill's back, but the bullet had damaged nothing more vital than a bottle of Navy rum which Bill was taking ashore.

The pair of them had wangled the job of manning one of the bridge oerlikon guns on the *Durban Castle* and so had enjoyed the naval privilege of a rum ration not vouchsafed to the rest of us.

As the sun was drying out our still damp clothing, men from other troops started to move up and down the track, and we began to receive driblets of information about the Commando's exploits. Casualties had been light and largely confined to A Troop and HQ Troop (where the second-in-command and the colonel's orderly had been amongst those killed). The Punta Castellazzo gun-emplacement had been taken at bayonet point but not without cost. One Italian had surrendered with a grenade in his hand but hadn't lived to see it explode. It was said that the comparative lack of opposition had been due to the local commander's decision to stand his men down in the belief that the prevailing sea conditions made a landing impossible. Whatever the reason, we had no complaints on that score, nor were we worried about the apparent boobs of Intelligence concerning Q House, the 'cliffs' and the other things which hadn't been quite in accordance with the briefing. What had happened to the building by the coastal track, and the track itself? Neither of these had been where expected. It may have been that we weren't put ashore precisely where anticipated, but those things didn't concern us at the time and we had neither the opportunity nor the desire to pursue them.

As we lay there, another of No. 41's Troop commanders, Captain Cunningham, a brother of 'Catseyes' Cunningham the RAF night-fighter ace, walked down the track heading back for medical treatment, clutching his shattered left elbow. We also learned, although this may have been at a later date, that the touchdown of the first Allied troops to return to Europe and stay there was at precisely 2.46 a.m., but we never discovered who had made a note of the fact.

It transpired that our Captain Stott, along with the other half of Q, had missed the landing altogether. Their LCA was found to have developed engine trouble as soon as it hit the water, and they had had to be taken back on board the *Durban Castle*. This explained the delay in starting our run in. They caught up with us about twenty minutes after the success signal, and it was clear that 'Stottie' was still hopping ('stotting'?) mad that the invasion had gone ahead without him. He was bursting to get into the war, so our stand-easy came to an abrupt end: 'Out pipes! On your feet!'

We shouldered our burdens and trudged off up the track. In minutes we were covered with a fine white dust which rose in clouds at each step of our marching feet. It settled into every crease and fold of uniforms and equipment and quickly combined with the sweaty oozings from under our steel helmets to make a muddy mess on our faces.

The countryside wasn't at all as we had imagined it. Instead of the luxuriant vegetation assumed to be the lot of every Mediterranean country, we found ourselves in a parched, dust-covered land. The expanses of lowly vines looked, at a distance, no more attractive than turnip fields, while the lines of cactus, interspersed with almond trees, did little to beautify the landscape – and everything within a dozen yards of the track was heavily coated with the white limestone dust. As we moved further up the rising ground, we were able to look back towards the Canadian landing-beaches. The sea, which only a few hours earlier had been dark, inhospitable and storm-tossed, was now as smooth as a sheet of glass, scintillating in the bright sunshine. Instead of a few small LCAs buffeting their way towards the shore, the whole seascape was now dotted with dozens of ships and landing-craft of all descriptions, some nosed up onto the beach, others extending far out towards the horizon. We turned our faces inland and pressed on, reassured by the knowledge that there would soon be a heck of a lot of people coming along behind us.

When we started off, the sun had been hot by our accustomed British standards and, as the morning advanced, it became progressively hotter. We marched and stopped, then marched again, responding to orders passed down the column, without knowing where we were going or why. At times we left the dusty tracks and moved across country in a long game of follow-my-leader that steadily became more and more sweaty, uncomfortable and tiring. On one occasion we passed a group of Italian civilians standing beside a few small cottages. They waved happily and treated us to cheerful grins but, while acknowledging their greeting, we couldn't help feeling that perhaps they had more to smile about than we had.

At one halting-place we found ourselves close beside a patch of watermelons just waiting to be 'liberated' and, after gorging ourselves on the fruit, were, happily, left alone long enough to enjoy a short snooze in the shade of a clump of trees. Roused reluctantly, we continued to march and by mid-afternoon were surprised to find ourselves slogging through a dank, muddy and definitely dismal stretch of woodland. It was a relief, after about half an hour, to emerge once more into the hot, bright sunshine. Apart from those few civilians encountered during the morning, Q Troop could have been the only living creatures in a deserted world. No sign of life nor any sound of war disturbed our lonely sweating until quite late in the afternoon.

We were then tramping along a good metalled road and, from a short distance ahead, heard the all-too-recognizable thumps of exploding mortar bombs. The volume of noise increased as we approached until, within a few hundred yards of where things were happening, our column was directed through an opening in a hedge on the left of the road. At the far end of the field in which we found ourselves, less than a hundred yards away, stood a single-storeyed, stone-built farm building which was acting as a buffer between us and the forward positions of the Commando where the bombs were landing. Casualties were being brought back to our side of the farm to have their wounds dressed before being passed down the medical line towards the beach. We knew that Italian mortars were larger than the Commando's three-inch weapons and could out-range them by about a thousand yards. There was little that our forward Troops could do other than 'take it', while ensuring that no infantry were following up the salvoes of bombs, until some heavier

Alec Kennedy, killed in action
at Salerno, 10 September 1943

The author with his brother, Lawrence, who was in the
Merchant Navy (August 1945)

'Geordie' Swindale, killed in action at Lion-sur-Mer on D-Day, June 1944

Harry Weiss, the Troop sniper, and Bill Marshall – 'The Terrible Twins' – outside their billet at Troon in May 1943 just before going overseas to Sicily

Officers of 41 Commando taken on board the *Durban Castle*
en route to Sicily:

Names left to right–

Lts. J. P. Salzberger (wounded Salerno), P. F. H. Wray (mentioned in despatches, killed Salerno), C. H. M. Sharpe (wounded Salerno), J. S. Stewart (wounded Salerno), A. D. Rolland, J. B. Williams (wounded Salerno), L. R. Scott (killed Salerno), C. E. Walker (wounded Salerno).

Regt. Sgt.-Maj. N. Tierney (missing presumed killed Salerno mentioned in despatches posthumously), Lt. W. J. M. Cooper (wounded Sicily), Capts. R. M. Stott (killed Salerno), H. E. Stratford, MC (wounded Salerno), A. D. Wilkinson (wounded Salerno), J. A. Taplin (wounded Sicily), W. Cunningham, DSO (wounded Sicily), Lt. W. D. Grant.

Surg.-Lieut. E. O. Davies, RNVR, Major J. McCann, 2nd i/c (killed Sicily), Lt.-Col. B. J. D. Lumsden, Commanding Officer (wounded Salerno), Capt J. R. Edwards, Adjt. (killed Salerno), The Revd. J. C. Wallis, RNVR

Lts. J. G. Burton, D. C. Lloyd (killed Salerno), M. G. Harvey (killed Sicily), P. H. Haydon, DSO (wounded Salerno), W. A. C. Horsfall (wounded Salerno).

Not in photograph—Capts. F. O. Ford (killed Sicily), S. C. Hellis, Administrative Officer, Lt. (QM) F. V. Borret, Quartermaster.

First Reinforcement: Capt J. F. Parsons, MC, Lt. J. S. Hawkard (killed Salerno).

Seaforth Highlanders boarding LCIs for the Sicily landing.
No. 299 also carried part of 41 Commando to Salerno

Grim-faced Commandos wait to go
ashore from an LCA

weapons could be brought to bear. Q Troop was being held in reserve, and we were ordered to dig in.

Our only means of excavation was the humble entrenching tool, a rather diminutive implement with a steel head, forged into the shape of a small, pointed fireside shovel at one end and a six-inch 'pick' at the other, which slotted onto a fifteen-inch-long wooden haft. We each carried one of these, along with all our other impedimenta, and were soon to become experts in their use. The ground was stony and baked hard with the sun, so the digging was slow and continued well into the evening, by which time the mortar fire had lapsed into desultory, sporadic salvoes and no other military activity had ensued.

Our holes were virtually finished when we were heartened by the clatter of tank tracks coming up the road behind us. 'Hurrah!' we thought. 'The tank lads will soon flush out those Eyetie mortars!' We waited expectantly but, when the thing came into view (and there turned out to be only one), our jaws dropped open in amazement. A tank it certainly was but not of any type we had seen before – so diminutive and nondescript that it looked as if the Canadian infantrymen had made it themselves. We gave it an ironic cheer as it passed. It continued up the road as far as the farm building, but at that point the driver must have decided that he really shouldn't have been there at all, because it immediately slewed round on its tracks and scuttled back the way it had come – to the accompaniment of a gale of incredulous laughter. Before darkness fell we received permission to brew up and put aside entrenching tools to occupy ourselves with tommy cookers and mess-tins. The menu was restricted: most of us opted for corned beef and biscuits, washed down with compo tea, before preparing to settle down for the night in our newly excavated holes.

With darkness came the start of the anticipated enemy air attacks on the landing-beaches and invasion fleet. Almost simultaneously, we were called from our foxholes by Sergeant Shepherd's stentorian command, 'All right! On your feet! Get rigged! We're moving off!' Our digging efforts had been for nought, and any hopes of a night of undisturbed sleep were dashed. We formed up quickly and marched off in single file across the road, then down the hillside to the right of the farm building. We tramped to the accompaniment of racing aero-engines, whistling bombs and the bright, crackling flashes of exploding anti-aircraft shells, all set against a wide backcloth of dark sky and probing searchlights. After the initial, relatively speedy descent of the hill, our progress became slow and intermittent. With no inkling of the where and whyfore of our journey, we subsided into the standard night-march routine of merely following the man in front, stopping when he stopped and moving on again when he rose to his feet. It must have been close to midnight – the enemy airmen had long since gone to their beds – when we finally halted just below the crest of a hill and were motioned to gather round. In a hushed whisper, the Troop commander put us in the picture.

An Italian counter-attack was likely during the night or at dawn next morning, and their anticipated line of advance would probably involve this particular piece of high ground. It would be critical for the whole invasion if the enemy were to break through to the beaches, so this could not be allowed to happen. They must not pass this point. There was to be no withdrawal. The hill must be defended to the last man!

After that cheering piece of information, we crept quietly over to the forward slope to prepare for the attack. We were allocated firing-positions in groups of three, in order to share the night watches on a one-hour-on and two-off basis, and told to get digging – but quietly! Wielding entrenching tools so as not to make a noise is not easy, and we soon found that, in that particular location and without any criteria for quietness, even full-sized picks and shovels would have been useless, as we hit bedrock within only a few inches of the surface. This initiated an immediate change from digging to raising breastworks around the shallow depressions we had managed to scoop out of the ground. Fortunately the hillside was littered with chunks of whitish rock which were just visible in the darkness, and our position soon resembled nothing so much as a disturbed ants' nest, with dozens of shadowy figures scurrying back and forth, carrying lumps of rock cradled in their arms or rushing around to find some more. It wasn't a heavy type of rock, probably a pumice or tufa, and its efficacy in stopping bullets was questionable, but it was that or nothing.

Our defences were taking shape when Captain Stott ordered Sergeant Shepherd to take out a reconnaissance patrol and probe forward of our position to determine whether there were any of the enemy in the immediate vicinity. I heard my name whispered – the tommy-gun had singled me out as first scout. Off I went, bent low, creeping slowly and silently down into the blackness below. At the limit of visibility, which was only a matter of yards, I paused to allow the second scout to reach my side, then moved off again while he remained, rifle at the ready, covering me, until I stopped again. The rest of the patrol (the section sergeant and three more riflemen) brought up the rear, catching up with the second scout every time I crept forward.

This, the standard scouting procedure, was repeated time and again as we made our slow progress down the hillside. In the darkness it was easy to persuade yourself that some of the shadows were moving figures, that each tree concealed a crouching enemy soldier or that every clump of bushes could very well be a squad of Italian infantry. At the foot of the hill, perhaps 600-700 yards from our starting-point, I crawled through a hedge and followed it slowly to the right along level ground for a few hundred yards more until the sergeant decided that there were probably no Italians in the neighbourhood and we retraced our steps to the Troop position.

Each three-man hole was now a distinct and separate entity in which, for what remained of the night, one man remained awake and on watch while the other two curled up behind their wall of stones. After the previous night's activities we were badly in arrears of sleep, so, notwithstanding the rocky beds, had no difficulty in dropping off. The tired man on watch, with eyelids desperately wanting to drop shut and stay closed, wasn't always completely certain whether a movement he had seen was real or imaginary. More than once our sleep was shattered by a rough shake and a hoarse urgent whisper, 'Hey! Wake up! Is that something moving to the left down there?' Even when three pairs of eyes were staring intently into the night, it was difficult to convince yourselves that the 'enemy' was nothing more than a bush or a rock.

Long before there was any perceptible lightening of the sky, Captain Stott moved from hole to hole making the last of the night rounds and ensuring himself that everyone was wide-awake and stood to, ready to receive a dawn attack. Crouching behind the breastworks, we waited expectantly. Lying silent and motionless, our muscles became stiff and cramped as, with irritating gradualness, the dawn of a new day transformed the menacing no man's land of the night into the vines, bushes and trees of a quiet Sicilian landscape. Were the Italians going to come in with the dawn? Ever so slowly the sky grew brighter – all about us remained quiet and peaceful. The sun had climbed well above the tree-tops before it was finally accepted that there was not going to be an attack upon our position. The Napoli Division seemed to have disappeared with the darkness, and the Troop was allowed to stand down, to flex cramped muscles, talk and smoke. Soon we had abandoned the holes and were gathered around a well which had been located in the valley immediately below our position, washing and shaving as though it was just another 'stunt' on the Isle of Wight.

We realized that it was Sunday morning, but our day of rest didn't last for long. After breakfasting on biscuits, cheese and jam, we moved off. Once again, for the whole of the day, we marched and sweated in the burning sun or dozed in whatever shade was available, if the stops became in the least protracted. For the most part our route lay along deserted minor roads, and as on the previous day we were in complete ignorance of our position, of the reason for our footslogging and of the whereabouts of the enemy. We knew that we were supposed to be protecting the left flank of the Canadians, so presumably they were somewhere to our right, but we saw neither hide nor hair of them nor of any other living creature. Once again we were moving in complete isolation.

At one point we passed some evidences of war – the bloated corpses of a few Italian soldiers, together with the carcases of their horses, all strewn together along the roadside amongst the shattered wreckage of two or three wooden carts. Nearby, the fields were spotted with dead cows, all swollen and stiff-legged. These were soon left behind and we tramped on through an empty countryside that continued to be dried up and dusty, unmarked and unremarkable. As there was no sign of the Italian Army, we could only assume that they were more accustomed to their own climate and so could march more quickly than we – or maybe they had got hold of some means of transport faster than horses and carts.

In the evening we were halted and ordered to dig in for the night, still not knowing where anybody was. When darkness fell, my tommy-gun once again earned me a place on a reconnaissance patrol. This time it was a larger and more protracted affair. A dozen of us moved forward from the Troop position with the job of carrying out a wide, clockwise sweep of about three miles, which alternated between cross-country work and stretches along well-paved roads. As on the previous night, we didn't encounter any of the enemy, and the patrol passed entirely without incident. After about an hour we returned to the Canadian lines some two miles from the Commando position. Our need for safe passage through the FDL (Forward Defended Locality, the technical term for what is commonly called 'the front line') had been advised to the Army unit through whose area we were to pass. They were expecting us, so a whispered exchange of passwords in the darkness was sufficient to give us safe re-entry into the bosom of the invasion forces.

That any unexpected approach to the forward areas, from no man's land, could be an extremely risky business was tragically brought home to us when we regained the Troop position. During our absence the Troop sergeant major had been killed in just such circumstances, by one of our own men. The sergeant major had apparently gone forward of the Commando position to draw water from a nearby well, without informing anyone. On his return he had been seen but not recognized in the darkness and for some unaccountable reason had not responded to the challenge. A marine had opened fire, killing him instantly. This episode didn't help our peace of mind for the remainder of that particular night, as we had been warned of reports that Italians had been caught creeping stealthily into Allied positions to knife our soldiers as they slept. In the event, the night passed quietly, with no untoward incidents.

Next morning we learned that the Canadians had captured Pachino and that they felt quite capable of taking care of their left flank by themselves. The Commando was to move to a 'rest area' to await further employment. A grave for the sergeant major was dug in a quiet corner formed by two tall hedgerows, and after the padre had performed the burial service, we set off in what we took to be the general direction of Pachino. It was another hot and dusty march but shorter this time, as it came to an end early in the afternoon. Our allotted bivouac area was in a lemon grove adjacent to an abandoned farmstead, and a reconnaissance of the outbuildings soon ended with another 'Success!' signal – a large cask of wine had been located. There was a rapid scatter for mess-tins. It was rough, dry stuff but we were hot and thirsty and had no difficulty in persuading ourselves that liberated *vino* was much more palatable than sterilized water. Happily, the voices of authority were stilled – maybe they had found something else – for we were able to drink our fill, then crawl into the shade of the trees before becoming lost to the world.

It was about six o'clock in the evening when we were roused to organize the camp area and be detailed off for duty watches. By this stage of the invasion, the marching-order packs we had left behind on the *Durban Castle* should have caught up with us, but we were told that they had, temporarily, gone astray. For weeks afterwards we continued to receive assurances that they would eventually turn up, but we never saw them again. Nevertheless, there was some tangible proof that we were indeed in a 'rest' area – each man was issued with a blanket and a mosquito net. With the net slung between two convenient trees and a blanket ready to roll into, the *al fresco* bed looked very inviting – but first of all there had to be another patrol.

This time it was to investigate a report that a sniper was holed up in a farmhouse a few miles away. As dusk fell, a party of about fifteen of us set off in single file until we reached the edge of a large, sombre wood. There we spread out into extended line and began moving cautiously forward from tree to tree, carefully searching the undergrowth while at the same time trying not to make any noise. At the far edge of the wood, having found nothing *en route*, we dropped down behind a low, bushy hedge and peered through. Only yards away, standing out white and silent in the moonlight, was a group of farm buildings. Hardly had we realized that we had arrived at the place where the sniper was supposed to be hiding than a bullet zinged from the wood behind us and smacked into the wall of the farmhouse, sending a shower of mortar chips splattering onto the path below. A single shot, then absolute silence. Had our quarry left the farm? Was he now shooting at us from the rear? Lieutenant Lloyd sent part of the patrol back to search the wood again, left a covering party along the hedge line and led the rest of us forward to see about making an entry.

The main two-storeyed farmhouse immediately to our front presented nothing but a blank wall, devoid of any doors or windows. Leading from it to the right, however, but set back some twenty feet or so, was a long, single-storey extension. This had a large double door standing at a height of some three feet above the pathway from which it was approached by a steep concrete ramp. Examination of the door showed it to be solidly built and locked, so Lieutenant Lloyd decided to blow it open with a rifle grenade. We all moved back down the ramp, the officer to instruct the 'EY' rifleman, who was with the party in the wood, while the rest of us ranged ourselves along the wall of the main building ready to charge back up the slope as soon as the door had been blasted open.

An EY rifle was a standard 303-calibre Lee Enfield but with its breech area copiously bound about with wire to prevent it disintegrating when using the special 'ballistic' cartridge needed to propel a grenade. Its name was a contraction of 'EmergencY' – firing grenades apparently caused such havoc to the barrel of the rifle that it was not to be used with ball ammunition except in an emergency. The recoil of firing a ballistic cartridge would break the shoulder of anyone unwise enough to discharge the EY in that position so, when firing grenades, the rifle was held with its butt planted firmly on the ground – and usually 'on its back', with the muzzle pointing in the required direction.

Fitted to the muzzle of the EY was a steel cannister just large enough to keep the firing-handle safely in position against the body of the grenade when it had been slipped in with the pin removed. When the trigger was actuated (with a push of the thumb rather than a squeeze of the fingers), the blast of the ballistic cartridge would eject the grenade from the cannister, allowing the firing-handle to fly clear. This released the spring-loaded firing-pin, allowing it to strike the percussion cap. The grenade was then 'live' as it curved through the air, all set to explode after the fixed time-setting of the fuse.

Crouching against the farmhouse wall, we heard the thump of the EY being fired, followed a second or so later by the thud of the grenade striking the door, smack on target. Then came dull, metallic noises which told us that the grenade had dropped onto the concrete ramp and was starting to roll down towards us. For a split second the absence of an explosion was puzzling – then the truth suddenly flashed through our minds: *a seven-second fuse!* Grenades to be thrown by hand were primed with a four-second fuse, but for the increased range achieved by a rifle it was usual to allow seven seconds.

As the rolling grenade gathered momentum, we guessed that it would be down on the path beside us before exploding, and there was a mad scatter for safety.

Those nearest the ramp threw themselves back into the wood; the rest could only flatten to the ground, bare milliseconds before the shattering burst of the explosion. Amazingly, not one of us was hit by any of those few dozen pieces of lethal metal flying about our heads, but they did provide ample reasons for trying a more normal means of gaining access. We trooped around to the front of the building and hammered on the farmhouse door with rifle butts.

Almost immediately a crowd of jabbering Sicilian women swarmed out, their waving arms adding weight to incomprehensible words. By this time, on the strength of my brief attempt at speaking Italian outside Q House, I was branded as the language expert – to be left outside to calm the ladies while the rest of the patrol went inside to search for the sniper. As on the previous occasion, the women were pleased to echo my '*Amici*'s but it seemed pointless to repeat the '*Non abbiate paura*' bit, as they gave the impression of being much more annoyed than afraid. After a fruitless search, the others rejoined me in the farmyard and, as those who had been sent back to search the wood had also drawn a blank, we returned to the bivouac area empty-handed. Nevertheless, it proved to have been a useful reconnaissance patrol. We returned next morning with Geordie Swindale, our unofficial 'handler', to liberate two of the farm's horses, together with a cart to carry some of the heavier equipment.

'Geordie' was not one of Marine Swindale's given names, just an indication that, like myself, his place of origin was Tyneside. We were, so far as I was aware, the only two from that part of the country in the Commando – although from different sides of the river: I lived in Newcastle, while Bill came from Windy Nook, Gateshead. Bill was a butcher by trade but had a fund of unlikely stories about his moonlighting job assisting the local undertaker. He was invariably cheerful, always ready to do a good turn, a real salt-of-the-earth Geordie, with an accent to match. My own accent wasn't quite so pronounced as Bill's, and on that account alone I would sometimes be referred to as 'the educated Geordie'. This soubriquet was intended neither as a compliment nor as an insult: it was no more than a jocular way of differentiating between the two of us, although I suspect that many of the unit believed that the two words 'educated' and 'Geordie' were a contradiction in terms.

The Commando remained in that rest area for only two days, and most of the time was spent in cleaning ourselves and our weapons. At one of the weapons inspections, Bill Smith and Betsy managed to draw attention to themselves for a second time – but for a reason entirely different from that in front of the Casa della Marza. This time, instead of failing to fire when she should have done so, Betsy loosed off a round when she shouldn't have. Bill had committed the cardinal sin of leaving a cartridge in the breech, so, when he smartly closed his gun after having had it inspected by Captain Stott, a bullet tore its way through the lemon trees – fortunately there was no one in the way. Not only had Betsy to be cleaned again but Bill was put on a charge and forfeited three days' pay.

We foraged the surrounding countryside in the hope of supplementing our rations but with little success. It was early in the season for oranges, and there seemed to be few ripe melons in our area, but we did locate some well-laden plum trees. As we were harvesting the fruit, a middle-aged Sicilian bustled out of a nearby house, waving his arms in great concern. 'Hey!' he shouted. 'What you tink you do? I spend-a-plenty-a money growin' de fruit!' It was pure comic-strip Italo-English. It transpired that he had lived in Brooklyn for a number of years, but we didn't consider that that was sufficient reason for us to forgo his plums. In our view he was extremely lucky to have 'plenty-a money', and if his German friends hadn't started the whole war business, we wouldn't have had any reason to be in his garden.

By this time the rations we had carried ashore were finished and we were on 'compo' (an abbreviation of 'composite'), a stiff, wooden-framed hardboard box containing a full day's ration of food (with the solitary exception of water) for fourteen men. There were in addition a few other creature comforts – a cigarette ration of seven per man, matches, chocolate or boiled sweets and toilet paper. Apart from the last-named, everything was packed in tins, and the heart of every box was a large, square tin of biscuits. These were of a hard cracker type consistency and took the place of bread and potatoes, as well as acting as general filling material when all else had been eaten.

There were seven basic menus for the main meal of the day, and these were indicated by reference letters stencilled on the outside of the boxes. Thus 'B' might indicate pork hash and marmalade pudding, while an 'F' would warn you of corned beef and rice pudding. The most sought-after was box 'A', which offered the delicacies of steak-and-kidney pudding followed by mixed fruit pudding. However, in view of the long journey each box had to make from the DID (Divisional Issuing Depot), very few of those collectors' items managed to get down as far as sub-section level. Breakfast would be either tinned bacon or tinned sausages – both in rather parsimonious portions, and for the rest it was biscuits with butter, jam and/or cheese. As for drinks, the one and only option was 'compo tea'. This could be a reasonable drink but it often turned out to be an unattractive, curdled, dust-covered concoction which, when brewed with salty Sicilian water, ended up being virtually undrinkable.

Despite all the potential drawbacks of that particular variety of the British national beverage, the invariable maxim of the armed forces at that time remained, 'When in doubt, brew up!' The mobile elements were in a particularly favourable position in that respect as they possessed both the essential fuel and the means of transportation of what was the nub of the whole tea-making business, the Benghazi cooker or Benghazi burner. This was no more than a tin (the biscuit tins from compo rations were quite suitable) punctured with a few air holes around the top edge and partially filled with sand or soil. After dowsing it with petrol and setting it alight, you were in business. A wire carrying-handle was essential, as it was often necessary to move off before the thing had cooled down, and it also enabled it to be hooked onto a vehicle. Everything that moved – tanks, trucks, jeeps, utilities, ambulances, staff cars – had a Benghazi cooker dangling from it somewhere. Another biscuit tin from the compo rations would often be used as the dixie in which to boil the water.

While we were in that rest area, the condition of the marine who had killed the sergeant major rapidly worsened. At night, under the combined effects of *vino* and remorse (the two men had been close friends), his shouting and sobbing could be heard throughout the Troop area. After the second night it was clear that he was in need of medical attention, and he was taken back to the beachhead.

On that day, too, we were told that the second phase of the Commando's role in the Sicilian operation – being based upon assault ships as a mobile landing force – was to be put into effect and that there was already a job lined up for us.

We would move off next day.

6 *Destroyer Trip and Assault Ship*

Immediately after breakfast on 15 July, we kitted up and left the lemon grove. Once again the sun was blazing hotly from the cloudless blue sky and, marching along another deserted country track, we were very soon in our accustomed hot, sticky and dusty condition.

After little more than an hour we reached an asphalt highway where we were halted beside the ruins of a solitary shell-shattered building. Here we were fallen out and told we were to await transport which was on its way to take us to the beach where there was a vessel ready to take us to the assault ships. We propped our weapons against the heaps of rubble and settled down in the ruins, hugging such meagre shade as the remaining stumps of walls provided. For the next few hours we endured one of those incomprehensible and invariably unexplained periods of waiting around which were so much a part of Service life.

It was long past noon before a string of Army three-tonners eventually arrived. We climbed aboard with a happy mixture of relief at being on the move again and curiosity about seeing some more of the country we had invaded. On top of that there was also a feeling of elation at the prospect of having our first ride on Italian soil and, in particular, at the idea of actually being carried around instead of having to propel ourselves.

After only a few miles our convoy entered Pachino, the town which had so dominated the ship-board briefings. The trucks made an almost complete circuit of the market square, which was thronged with people who watched our progress with obvious interest but no great enthusiasm. For our part we were eager to see the results of the RAF's visitations on the night of the landing, and we rubber-necked around looking for signs of damage – but without success. So far as we could make out, the place was completely untouched. What did impinge upon our eyes, however, was the repetition, *ad nauseum*, of the single word '*Salone*'. It seemed to be carried by about one in four of the numerous shops flanking the square, and even the least linguistically inclined amongst us realized that it must mean 'Saloon'. Lips were licked appreciatively until the more perceptive types deduced that these were no *vino* dens but hairdressing establishments.

About ten minutes after leaving Pachino we arrived at a long stretch of beach where some of the main Eighth Army landings had taken place. It was still a vast area of urgent activity as more and more supplies were being brought ashore. For the first time, we foot-sloggers gained some inkling of the colossal logistics problems involved in satisfying the everyday needs of tens of thousands of troops. The sandy soil immediately behind the beach was groaning under immense stacks of petrol, food, munitions of all kinds and goodness knows what else, all neatly arranged in amazingly long, orderly rows and draped with camouflage netting. On the beach itself, heavily laden trucks with engines racing in low gear ploughed their way through the soft sand as they brought further loads to the stockpiles. Behind the beach there were more loaded vehicles churning away at the start of their trips up to the forward areas, while strings of 'empties' were returning to join the line of those awaiting their turn to be re-filled.

Here and there bulldozers of the Royal Engineers were levelling more sand dunes while squads of men, stripped to the waist, sweated as they positioned sections of Somerfeld interlocking steel tracking to form more access roads across the foreshore. On the sparkling and almost painfully inviting calm blue sea, landing-craft of all descriptions, including the recently perfected amphibious

DUKWs,* were plying to and fro as they ferried ashore ever more materials of war from the numerous supply ships anchored in deeper water. After our lonely, dusty days tramping through a deserted countryside, this panorama of bustling activity presented us with a new and enthralling aspect of the invasion business.

Amongst the merchant ships, but closer inshore, lay the sleek British destroyer which was to take us to our rendezvous with the assault ships. Landing-craft were beached, ready to carry us out to her, and in a matter of minutes we were scrambling up the boarding-nets and onto the deck of HMS *Quantock*. As soon as all were on board, the destroyer weighed anchor and raced off up the coast. We were told that a diversion behind the enemy lines had already been planned for that very night, so time was short.

The sailors welcomed us with liberal hospitality. Their mess decks, small and cramped even for the normal ship's complement, were now overflowing with hundreds of dusty and dishevelled marines. A continuous flow of kettles of tea – real tea this time – began to arrive from the galley and, after having had to make do with empty food tins for the past few days, it was a luxury to be able to drink out of a civilized enamel mug. No official food had been provided but, from their personal supplies, the matelots produced bread (another luxury), butter, tinned meat, bars of chocolate and cigarettes. We also made good use of their 'ablutions' for a clean-up and to pour away the salty, chlorinated water and refill our bottles from the much more palatable ship's supply. We were given pencils and paper to scribble letters home and were

---

* Factory code letters to indicate year of manufacture and construction details of a six-wheeled American amphibious vehicle produced by General Motors: D – 1942, U – Utility (Amphibian), K – All-wheel drive, W – Dual rear axles. By some unlikely coincidence the letters almost produce the name of the creature the craft so closely resembled and by which they were invariably known – DUCKS. They were capable of carrying 30 armed men or 2½ tons of supplies at 50 mph on land or 5 mph in water, and were first used in Sicily.

assured that they would be on their way to the UK that same evening, compliments of the Navy. After the sweat, dust and flies ashore, it was like being in a seventh heaven to lie on the pleasantly warm, pulsating deck, replete and reasonably clean, dreaming of being blue marines who were spending *their* war on floating hotels like this. The speeding warship, cutting its way through the placid sea, created a cooling breeze which tempered the heat of the sun and pushed everything from our minds but the huge enjoyment of the sea trip.

The end came all too quickly. After less than two hours we felt the racing engines slacken speed and roused ourselves to move across to the port side to see what was happening. With some dismay we found that we were already surprisingly close to a waterfront of multi-coloured buildings. This, the sailors assured us, was Syracuse. As the destroyer was nosing its way, slow ahead, into the harbour, already well filled with shipping tied up at the quays and anchored in the fairway, news filtered through that the assault ships had been delayed, so the landing arranged for that night had been postponed for twenty-four hours. There wasn't sufficient room on board to accommodate us overnight, so we were to be put ashore to fend for ourselves. When the *Quantock* was eased alongside the quay, we thanked our generous hosts for the trip and trooped down the gangway to form up on the quayside.

The whole dock area was a shambles of bomb-blasted buildings and rubble-strewn roadways, all covered with the now familiar white dust. There was no way of telling whether the devastation had been the work of the RAF during the invasion or the Italians attacking our ships afterwards, but it didn't really matter. 'Move to the right in threes!' Off we marched – but for only a few hundred yards, when we were fallen out again beside the wreck of the dockside railway station. We settled down on the platforms, amongst the twisted steel skeleton and splintered glass of the station roof, for another period of unexplained waiting. The whole area reeked of desolation, destruction and 'DOOCHAY'. Words of adulation for 'Il

Duce', Mussolini, were plastered in any direction we cared to look. Such walls of the station building as were still standing bore neatly scripted quotations from his speeches, while the single word *'Duce'*, repeated, *ad infinitum* in letters five or more feet high, screamed down at us from virtually every gable end of the houses which rose, tier upon tier, above the docks.

Shadows were lengthening when we each received a tin of M & V (Meat and Vegetables) for our evening meal, and sleeping-quarters were allocated. Q Troop was assigned to the docks' post office, a bombed-out shell of a building of which no more than a portion of the ground floor remained reasonably intact. Its interior was a jumbled maze of shattered masonry, plaster, rubble, broken glass, mangled office equipment and undelivered mail.

One interesting find was a pile of British newspapers dated June 1940, which had obviously never been read and were still almost as good as new. Presumably they had arrived in Syracuse just as Italy decided to enter the war and had never been forwarded to the newsagents. We soon tired of straining our eyes in the half-light, trying to read news items that were some three years old, but the papers came in useful for softening our rubbly beds. Some of us decided that the best place to sleep would be under the post-office counters where less debris had accumulated. In spite of being slightly claustrophobic, the stout woodwork would provide some protection should anything untoward happen.

As had been expected, darkness brought out the enemy bombers and, for good measure, we were told that Intelligence had dreamed up the possibility of Syracuse's being attacked by parachutists that night. As the only ground troops in the area, we had been given the honour of providing the anti-parachutist defence of the town.

The first duty watch of the Troop went out into the streets, and the rest of us crawled into the inky darkness beneath the post-office counters. As the first wave of bombers came over, every gun in the area, on ship and shore, must have opened up – from 4.7 inch ack-ack guns, down through all the smaller calibres to multiple pom-poms and 20 mm oerlikons. We could hear them spraying the sky with high explosives and hot steel. Added to all of this came the scream of aero-engines, the whistle of falling bombs and the jolting crashes as they exploded. The resulting cacophony engendered conditions that were not particularly conducive to sleep, but we managed it, somehow. Unfortunately it didn't last long. We awakened, coughing and spluttering in a dense fog of acrid smoke. With eyes streaming, throats dry and sore, we groped our way through the blackness of the post-office building and out into the street. But there we found that conditions were only marginally better: the whole dock area had been blanketed under a dense smoke-screen put down by the Navy to hide the shipping from the bombers. This may very well have spoiled the airmen's aim and forced them to bomb at random, but it didn't deter them from coming back again and again.

It was unrealistic to imagine that parachutists would be dropped during an air raid, but we still had to go out into the town to keep watch, and our turn came just as the guns were building up to another crescendo. Moving through the dark and deserted streets to take up our positions, we were forced to dodge from doorway to doorway through a rain of jagged steel splinters from the bursting shells. The smaller pieces merely tinkled as they hit the roadway; the larger ones struck with a metallic clank that made you feel glad they had missed you, but the biggest chunks of all heralded their approach with a sort of 'wobbly whine' caused by their off-balance twisting and turning as they tore through the air before impacting with murderous thumps. We passed most of our tour of duty sheltering in doorways and, apart from the aerial activity, the night passed uneventfully.

At dawn the whole unit was stood to – just in case. We stayed on full alert until broad daylight, even though the last planes had disappeared long before the first greying of the sky. When it was finally decided that there wasn't going to be any attack, we were allowed an hour's sleep before breakfast.

After we had eaten and while awaiting the arrival of the

assault ships, it was a welcome surprise to be told we could wander off into the nearby streets if we wanted to, carrying only personal weapons, on a half-go, half-stay basis. When our turn came, it was another surprise to see the number of Italian civilians who were also moving around. Our brief acquaintanceship with Syracuse had given the impression that it was completely dead and deserted but we found that the streets were well populated. It was a new experience to be able to saunter around a 'conquered' town without having to wear any of our weighty equipment, thoroughly enjoying the warm sunshine and making pleasant 'How d'ye do!' inclinations of the head to anyone who seemed likely to respond.

The two previous attempts at speaking Italian must have gone to my head because, when I saw two uniformed Italians resplendent in shining plumed helmets approaching, I stopped in front of them and enunciated '*Che ora è, per favore?*' ('What time is it, please?') – and it worked! One of them reached into his pocket to extract a veritable turnip of a watch and answered. My knowledge of the language didn't extend to understanding what he said but it was enough to have verified that another phrase from the little handbook actually worked. I grinned and responded, '*Grazie!*'

The assault ships arrived in Syracuse harbour early that afternoon. They were the *Queen Emma* and the *Princess Beatrix*, two small, fast Dutch ships whose peace-time role had been crossing and re-crossing the North Sea between Britain and the Netherlands. Now, like the *Durban Castle*, they were armed and carried flotillas of LCAs. The Commando was split between the two ships, with Q Troop being detailed for the *Princess Beatrix*. Once on board, we were given a brief and very sketchy outline of the proposed operation.

The Commando was to be landed a few miles to the north of Catania, well behind the German lines, with the twofold purpose of creating a diversion (timed to coincide with a major push north by the Eighth Army) and interrupting road and rail traffic carrying supplies and reinforcements to the front. After taking up positions from which to deny the enemy the use of these supply routes, we would hold out until things became too hot. Then it would be a case of either returning to the beach for evacuation or, if that proved to be impossible, scattering into the countryside to hole up and await relief by the advancing British troops. In comparison with the detailed minutiae of the planning of the Sicilian landing, it appeared that this one was going to be something of a 'suck it and see' operation.

When the *Emma* and *Beatrix* sailed from Syracuse, we were again keyed up for action in a matter of hours. The ships steamed only a dozen miles or so, to Augusta, the next port up the coast, and anchored in the wide bay to while away the few hours to nightfall before making the last short approach trip to the selected landing-point. Then, without warning, the operation was OFF again! It was variously rumoured that this was just another twenty-four-hour postponement, to fit in with the Eighth Army's preparations for their attack, and that a German division had suddenly established a rest camp close to the place selected for our landing. Be that as it may, we were simply told to settle down for the night.

By this time we had discovered that living-space on the *Beatrix* was much more cramped than anticipated and had rather gone off the idea of living on a floating base. However, unlike the *Durban Castle*, bedding-down on deck was permitted, provided you didn't stray beyond the positions designated by the Navy. Most of those who wished to sleep in the open were able to find places where it was at least possible to stretch out full length. I joined a group of a score or more in what ended up as being a rather crowded location, largely roofed over by an upper deck but still open to the cool night air. There are softer beds than a steel deck, but for us it was sufficient to be free from such plagues as dust, mosquitoes and choking phosphorous smoke, so it didn't take long to fall into a deep sleep.

But it was too good to last! The raucous 'Kruaark! Kruaark! Kruaark!' of the ship's klaxon, summoning the off-duty watch to their action stations, jerked everyone into wakefulness. Sailors racing to man their guns had no time to pick a way through the recumbent forms of non-paying guests, and many a bruised and winded marine was left in the wake of their passing. We could hear the drone of aircraft engines coming uncomfortably close; then we heard the order to the guns' crews to 'Open fire!' The consequence was distinctly impressive. As on the previous night at Syracuse, every gun in the harbour area, on ship and shore, opened fire simultaneously, loosing off a tremendous quantity of shells, filling the night sky above us with an uproar of crackling explosions. Only then did we, on that particular area of deck, discover that we had something else to contend with. Unknowingly, our chosen sleeping-space lay directly beneath a multiple pom-pom mounting. As the gun opened fire with its four barrels, we began to vibrate in rhythm and, as it spewed its shells skywards at the rate of scores per minute, a continuous stream of empty shellcases clattered in a metallic cascade onto the steel deck above our heads.

Now dive-bombers roared down to the attack, loosing off screeching bombs which burst with violent concussions in the water around us. We lay helpless and half-deafened under a torrent of noise. At times the scream of a plane, in an almost vertical dive, would reach such a pitch that it seemed impossible that the pilot could ever pull out in time. On one such occasion we clearly heard a seaman above us shout, 'He's coming down the bloody funnel this time!' Then, with bombs released, the scream of the racing engine would change to a vicious snarl as the aeroplane zoomed up again to escape the concentrated curtain of flak, leaving us with the blast of exploding bombs and the disconcerting rolling of the ship when they had dropped unpleasantly close.

From beneath the pom-pom, we had only a restricted view of the night sky, towards the stern of the ship, but it was almost continually filled with action – swinging beams of searchlights, curving arcs of tracers and the flashes of exploding shells. More than once we felt thankful for the small mercy of not having to worry about falling shell splinters but weren't sure whether that was adequate compensation for the other problems. In the relatively few periods of calm, when our ships' guns were silent, we had no option but to eavesdrop on the comments of the sailors over our heads, 'There's the bastard again! Dead ahead! Let him have it!' – and the clanking splatter of shellcases would start again. Lying there, inactive and helpless, the succession of attacks seemed interminable, but gradually we realized that the periods of quietness were becoming longer, and at last all became peaceful again. The off-duty watch of the ship's crew was stood down. We, and they, returned to our interrupted sleep.

Not until the following morning did we learn that, although the *Beatrix* was unscathed, there had been almost a hundred casualties on the *Emma*. A very close near-miss had detonated mortar bombs and hand-grenades on the marines' mess deck. A few of the ship's complement had been involved but most of the casualties were Royal Marine replacements sent out from the UK to make up losses suffered during the Sicilian landing and had been with the Commando only a few days. Those of us who had hankered after the life of a shipboard marine – when lazing on the deck of HMS *Quantock* racing through the serene waters of the Mediterranean – now realized that there was quite a lot to be said for being stuck on shore. Foxholes were, if nothing else, unsinkable, and their occupants weren't greatly affected by near-misses provided they kept their heads down.

As the *Emma* limped away towards Malta with our dead and wounded, it became obvious that, as well as killing many of our men, that air raid had killed the idea of basing the Commando on assault ships. We were put ashore on a deserted quay, formed up in threes and, with our backs turned on the now shining and peaceful waters of Augusta harbour, marched quickly away. We tramped through the empty streets of the town, littered with rubble and lined with the gutted shells of buildings, then out into the sun-scorched but equally empty countryside beyond. At first it seemed as though the intention was to put as many miles as possible between us and the Mediterranean, but after an hour or two our progress seemed to lose all sense of purpose and became more and more spasmodic. By mid-afternoon it finally ground itself to a halt. This, we were told, was as far as we were going for the time being.

There was no sign of any human habitation, although, only a few hundred yards away, there stood an isolated, walled cemetery. Many of the headstones had settled into untidy, slouching postures which gave the place an aura of dilapidation and neglect. As we lowered our weapons and equipment to the ground, something much more interesting caught our eyes. Just beyond the cemetery, awaiting our attention, lay a large plot of melons – and ripe ones too. Pausing only to light cigarettes, we strolled across. At the same time, despite its seemingly remote situation, a line of scurrying figures appeared at the other side of the melon patch. We could hear their cries of, 'Mellone! Mellone!' as they alerted family and friends to gather in as much of the fruit as possible before it could be appropriated by the licentious soldiery. We managed to liberate enough for our immediate needs and, after being thus fortified, spent the next few hours in our usual evening excavation works.

Augusta was only a few miles away, so, as we settled down to sleep, we were able to watch the build-up of enemy air activity over the port without any concern about being involved in it ourselves. It was rumoured that, after the previous night's happenings, two anti-aircraft cruisers had been sent in to help protect the shipping. The intensity of the ack-ack barrage – which we could see in its entirety and watch with impunity – seemed to bear out the rumour.

Looking back with interest from our safe distance, most of us felt rather glad to be on dry land again. At least there was no restriction on the area of sleeping-space you could occupy, and each of us had his own individual hole into which he could pop should things get rough.

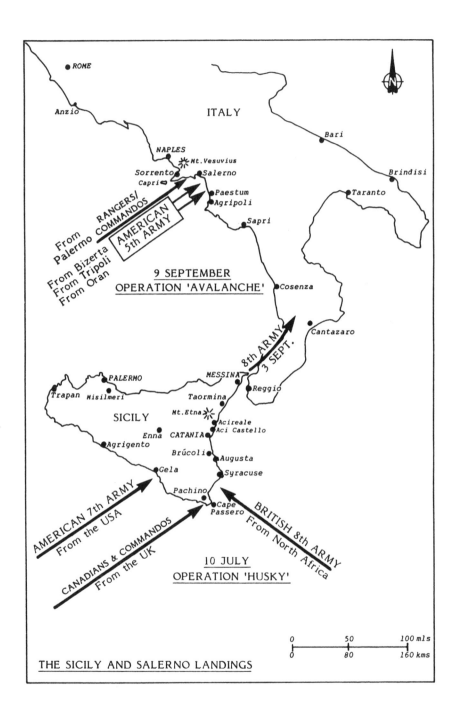

THE SICILY AND SALERNO LANDINGS

7 Rest Areas and Yankee Rations

Next morning, by which time – had the diversionary raid come off – we could have been lying low somewhere behind the German lines, we abandoned the holes beside the cemetery and marched off. Once more our tramping column meandered along dusty and deserted roads. A week had passed since the landing and, although the coastal highway was continually chock-a-block with an endless stream of guns, tanks and supply vehicles, we – only a few miles inland – were trudging through an empty landscape. The terrain was not unlike a dried-up version of British parkland; it exhibited no signs of war, apart from ourselves, and very little of the local population.

For most of the day our commanding officer was away at a conference, and endless buzzes about where we were headed and why and for how long passed interminably up and down the line. It was late afternoon before the CO returned with the news that we had been directed to another rest area to be held in readiness and await further developments. The Eighth Army's advance up the coast was meeting increasingly stubborn resistance – they were still some miles south of Catania, and it appeared that an appreciable period of build-up would be required before another push forward could be undertaken. On balance we were much happier with the idea of being held in readiness by General Montgomery, rather than lying in hiding somewhere up the north of Catania, awaiting his delayed arrival.

Our march ended near the village of Brúcoli standing on the high ground overlooking the Bay of Catania, some seven miles north of Augusta and about two miles from the sea. Once more we were assigned to a lemon grove, but a smaller and more secluded one this time. We began the inevitable digging operations but again found the depth of the soil to be less than a foot. This cut down the labour of excavation but meant that the resulting holes were likely to be of doubtful protection. (It seemed surprising that lemon trees could flourish in such shallow soil.) The exposed rockhead would not make very comfortable beds but, with the holes topped off with mosquito nets, our sleeping-quarters were ready for occupation.

When darkness fell, we weren't at all surprised when the stillness of the night was disturbed by the drone of approaching aircraft. We guessed that they were on their way to make another attack on the port of Augusta and paid little heed. But suddenly the whole bivouac area was illuminated as bright as day when a nearby searchlight battery switched on. Almost simultaneously the surrounding countryside burst into an uproar of crashing explosions and brilliant flashes as heavy anti-aircraft guns opened fire. We seemed to be surrounded by them, and it was revealed later that our hill was on the optimum run-in for enemy bombers heading for the port and shipping in the Bay of Augusta. We weren't troubled by any bombs but, as the guns hammered away at the bombers passing overhead, splinters of their shells sliced through the trees about us. To lie down in such circumstances would have been most unwise, so an appreciable part of each night had to be spent squatting under a mosquito net, trying to compress your whole body within the doubtful protection of a steel helmet.

It could very well have been no more than a coincidence that we had been deposited cheek by jowl with a combination of searchlights and ack-ack guns, but we did wonder whether there wasn't perhaps some jovial Army officer at Divisonal Headquarters who was able to regale his mess with the hilarious tale of the great rest area he had selected for a bunch of marines.

By day it was a completely different world. Then, the only sound of war to reach us was on those infrequent occasions when the wind carried the dull rumble of gunfire across the Bay of Catania from the front, some fifteen miles away. In the hot sunshine this meant no more to us than the noise of distant thunder. On only one occasion were we disturbed by enemy aircraft during the day, when a single Italian fighter roared down with guns blazing to strafe our bivouac, fortunately with no effect other than a rapid scatter for cover. The pilot must have had other things on his mind, as he didn't bother to return for a second attack.

Our stay at Brúcoli lasted almost three weeks. For the first few days we carried out extensive sweeps through the surrounding countryside, searching the scattered farms for concealed weapons. It didn't take long to discover that the gleaming white buildings which had looked so attractive on the briefing photographs were anything but clean and picturesque at close quarters. Nor had the photographs given any hint of the smells. At each farmhouse, which appeared to be shared on equal terms by animals and humans, we found trays of sliced tomatoes and other fruits spread out in the sun to dry – but no weapons. When we were not away searching farms, our mornings would be occupied in a variety of fatigue duties – ration parties, water parties or petrol-stacking parties.

At that time the British Army used a four-gallon petrol can, about ten inches square and a foot high, fabricated from very thin gauge tinplate. They had carrying-handles of spindly wire which were liable to pull off at the slightest provocation, and anything approaching rough handling would result in the cans developing leaks or even splitting apart at the seams. In view of their most obvious characteristics, they were invariably referred to as 'flimsies', and no one was sorry to see them replaced by an unashamed copy of the German model, the jerrican. The flimsies had at least one advantage: they could be stacked in neat, compact piles; this was occasionally one of our jobs, off-loading petrol trucks, then forming long rows of cans against the hedgerows and covering them with camouflage netting. On one of these petrol parties, shortly after our arrival at Brúcoli, we heard the unaccustomed whooping of a train whistle and rushed to the top of what we only then realized was a railway embankment, to see a diminutive steam-engine struggling to haul a long line of wagons piled high with war supplies for the front. Somehow it seemed to symbolize the fact that the Allied hold on Sicily was secure and would soon be complete. We instinctively gave a rousing cheer as it chuffed slowly past.

Water was quite a luxury, although it often had a distinctly salty taste due presumably to wells near the coast being contaminated by the infiltration of sea water. We drew our supplies from the well at a nearby farm that appeared to be used by most of the local populace for, at whatever hour you went to draw water, there would be an incredible number of people hanging around the farmyard – old men, women of all ages and droves of children. If not drawing water, they would be just sitting around in the sun – with hundreds of foreign soldiers living in shallow holes scooped out of their land, there was probably very little else they could do. We British invaders, who were required to behave like the war-time civilians back home and take our place in the queue, wondered whether German troops in our situation would have been ordered to do the same. There was little inclination on either side to 'fraternize' – although that particular word didn't come into general usage until the 1945 occupation of Germany.

Now that our lifestyle was more settled, communal arrangements were made to heat up the rations and brew the tea. With compo it was simply a matter of placing the tins in a dixie of water and boiling until the contents were heated through. Nevertheless, we always gave those responsible for the work the honorary title of 'cook'. They generally took their work seriously and invariably looked upon compo biscuits as a challenge. They tried a number of ways of making them more palatable, but neither 'biscuit porridge' (i.e. with milk, sugar and water added) nor 'biscuit soup' (made with the addition of water and meat extract) was anything more than wet, flavoured biscuits. Then we received some raisins as an 'extra', and the cooks decided to pull out all the stops. They would make a cake! An oven was built, using compo biscuit tins, and the mixture of biscuits, sugar, water and raisins was prepared in another tin and put in the oven to bake. It was a valiant effort but the result was perhaps predictable – a case-hardened biscuit exterior with a soggy mash of biscuits and raisins inside.

One of the inevitable and most frequent of our duties was to guard the bivouac area – and, more particularly, the compo rations, which were at risk from Italian civilians and Allied troops alike. Seven cigarettes per day wasn't a lot, even for a relatively light smoker, and each compo box held a hundred. You could generally manage to swap your sweet ration for the cigarettes of a non-smoker, but if you smoked and also had a sweet tooth, the ration boxes might be a temptation. It wasn't unknown to come across a seemingly intact box only to find that the cigarettes had been removed via a hole strategically cut in the side. Extra chocolate and the more popular meals, like steak-and-kidney pudding, were also much sought-after. In spite of their being covered with a tarpaulin sheet and watched by conscientious guards, it was a continuing problem.

So far as we were concerned, the ration box had to continue to provide us with crockery as well as food. The lack of mugs – gone astray with our big packs – meant that we had to use empty food cans as cups. This in itself wasn't a great hardship, nor were we very much concerned about the flying insects which managed to immolate themselves in our tea at every meal and had to be fished out before drinking. But this may have had some bearing on our continuing problem of dysentery. No one moved without his entrenching tool assembled and ready for action. Wherever you settled, it was close to hand. The calls of the affliction were so urgent and immediate that no apologies were expected when one of your number suddenly grabbed his entrenching tool and projected himself into the nearest foliage. On his rejoining the group there would be no comment, except perhaps, 'Come on! Stick or twist?' 1944 was probably a very good year for marsala in the Brúcoli region.

Much more than the enamel mugs, we missed our

change of clothing. Most servicemen had to acquire the skills of a laundryman in order to carry out their own 'dhobying', and with the continuing hot weather it wasn't too much of a problem to wash your underwear and get it back on again in a couple of hours or so. Our KSDs were a different matter: after three or four weeks of wearing them night and day, with only the earth as a mattress, they had become distinctly grubby.

From observation of the local ladies washing their clothes on the banks of a nearby stream, it was clear that they managed to turn out a sparkling wash simply by using rocks to pound out the dirt. All that was required was a bar of soap and a flat stone. So one afternoon I set out to emulate the signoras, experimenting on my bush jacket. There was no doubt that it was rendered cleaner but I must have employed much more exuberance than understanding because the overall effect was distinctly marred by a row of jagged holes across the shoulders.

The afternoons, when not detailed off for guard duties, were generally free and, despite the two-mile walk involved, the thought of a cool, cleansing swim in the Mediterranean was usually persuasive enough to start us off towards the sea. Having reached the rocky coast and actually frolicking in the cool, crystal-clear water, there were no doubts that the walk had been worthwhile. Afterwards, however, arriving back in camp just as hot and sweaty as when leaving, you weren't at all sure.

In addition to the hot walks back to camp, these swimming excursions could have two other drawbacks. One was the practice adopted by some members of the Armed Forces of fishing with hand-grenades. The explosion of a grenade thrown into the sea would result in dozens of dead and stunned fish floating up to the surface – all ready to be collected. But the concussion of the explosion was also felt by any human being in the water within a couple of hundred yards or so. Its effect wasn't quite so drastic as with the fish but it could still be equivalent to a hefty punch in the solar plexus. Much worse, however, were those occasions when, as you drew near to the sea, the onshore breeze brought the first tell-tale whiff of the stench of the partially decomposed carcase of some horse or mule which had floated inshore and become wedged in the rocks. Then there was absolutely no alternative but to return disconsolately to Brúcoli without even cooling your feet.

We weren't allowed to leave the bivouac area in the evening so any entertainment had to be in camp. Also, apart from those few occasions when we were able to purchase a bottle of doubtful marsala from an equally suspect Sicilian, there was no alternative but to provide our own. Anything singable was sung with gusto. Our repertoire included all the popular songs of the day, most of the World War I favourites, a selection of rollicking Salvation Army numbers (some with slightly modified lyrics) and a few Irish Rebel songs, such as 'Kevin Barry' and Bill Smith's solo turn, 'McCaffertay'. One of our star vocalists was a bren-gunner from No. 8 section with the appropriate name of Nightingale, but no evening was complete without a soulful rendering of 'Suvla Bay' by Corporal Matt Walsh. This sad song of the First World War, of an Australian girl who enters a convent after her fiancé had been killed in the ANZAC landings at Suvla Bay, Gallipoli, seemed to become 'our' song. We were still surprised at having had such a lucky break at Commando Cove and felt some kind of fellow feeling with that fictitious Aussie soldier who had been unfortunate enough not to survive *his* landing.

At dusk the concert would be terminated by the Troop sergeant, our muezzin of the 'Mepacrine Parade', bawling at us to get fell in. Every evening we had to parade in night order – that is, wearing long trousers (we of course had no alternative) with jacket sleeves rolled down to the wrist and shirts buttoned up to the neck. It was then that we each received – and had to be seen to swallow – a small yellow anti-malaria tablet of mepacrine, our second line of defence against the mosquitoes. 'Dismiss' generally coincided with the first drone of those other nocturnal flying things, the enemy bombers, and the ack-ack guns would start up.

Towards the end of our stay at Brúcoli we were

suddenly aroused during a night air raid with a call for volunteers to help the RASC load a train with petrol, urgently needed at the front. Some were sent up to the dumps to load trucks but I was assigned to the squad on the station platform, transferring the flimsies from truck to train. The German pilots seemed to have a suspicion that something was happening, for bombs which would normally have been carried all the way to Augusta were being dropped uncomfortably close to us. We sweated on the platform for about two hours, passing can after can after can into waiting hands within the trucks, trying hard not to think of what kind of a bonfire there would be if one of those bombs landed too close. When the very last flimsy had been passed on board and the long train puffed slowly away, we heaved sighs of relief and gave a parting salute of 'V' signs to the Service Corps men who were to travel with it.

On 5 August we learned that the Eighth Army, without any help from us, had pushed the Germans beyond Catania and was pursuing them in the direction of Messina. In the early hours of the following morning the Commando entrucked to tag along behind. After travelling a dozen miles through the typical tree-covered hills of coastal Sicily, we unexpectedly found our trucks rolling out onto the wide, open flatness of the Plain of Catania.

Passing from the dappled shade of the trees onto the exposed, bare expanse of sunbaked grass was an instantaneous transition from peace to war. Instead of trees, the road was now lined with twisted metal skeletons, the wrecks of 'soft' vehicles – trucks, utilities, jeeps, staff cars, both British and German, lying at the sides of the carriageway, where they had been driven or bulldozed off the metalling to clear a passage for others to move ahead. Away from the road, scattered far and wide across the vast area of the plain, were the knocked-out fighting vehicles – tanks, half-tracks and self-propelled guns, blasted and blackened where that last fatal bomb, shell or mine had brought them to a fiery end. Here, there and everywhere, low mounds of dry earth, marked with rough crosses or more often simply by a rifle, thrust muzzle-first into the ground, with a steel helmet draped over the butt, showed where the dead lay in their shallow graves. Some were quite alone but others lay in groups – a tank crew beside their trackless vehicle, a driver and his mate beside the scrap metal of their truck, British and German still distinguishable in death as in life by the shape of their helmets.

As the trucks trundled on, our attention became divided between this aftermath of the battle for Catania and the cone of Mount Etna, which grew more and more imposing as we neared the far side of the plain. A faint plume of steam issuing from its summit was evidence enough that, although quiescent, it was by no means extinct.

On reaching Catania, the trucks slowed down to a crawl, to negotiate the scattered heaps of rubble and abandoned military equipment littering the city streets. The main façades of the buildings seemed intact, although often slashed and pock-marked by shell-fire and bomb splinters. In a few places the rubble of a collapsed building had reduced the road width to a single lane but, compared with the wholesale devastation of parts of London, Catania was virtually untouched. There were very few Italians about to watch us pass, and we were probably the only ones to take any notice of the small groups of khaki-clad figures who were busy off-loading small groups of vehicles parked outside the various buildings which had already been commandeered for use as military headquarters or offices for AMGOT, the Allied Military Government of Occupied Territories.

Immediately beyond the city we found that peace had miraculously returned to the countryside. We bowled cheerfully along a road which alternated between shady wooded areas and stretches of bright sunshine giving tantalizing views of the sparkling Mediterranean. But after only half a dozen miles the convoy slowed and stopped; this was the end of the line so far as we were concerned. As soon as we had debussed, the trucks turned round and headed back the way they had come, no doubt to bring forward more troops or supplies.

For the remainder of the day we waited there by the roadside, apparently forgotten, while a continuous stream of military traffic rumbled past, heading north. Only when dusk was falling did the flow stop and all vehicles were driven off the road, parked nose to tail under the roadside trees and draped with camouflage netting. Everyone prepared to pass the night on the grass verge. Drivers and others travelling with vehicles had water for washing and shaving but we were spared such chores, making do with some cold compo and a can of tea for supper, plus the inevitable mepacrine tablet. Thereafter the road became something like a seaside promenade on a summer evening – lacking only the sea and the girls. For a couple of hours, hundreds of marines and a variety of soldiers strolled up and down the long line of camouflaged vehicles, swapping yarns and cigarettes in the warm darkness.

As we were curling up on the ground for sleep, from somewhere close by in the quiet stillness of the night a good Italian voice began singing 'O sole mio'. We listened in rapt attention as it was followed by a succession of similar Italian songs, all sung unaccompanied and apparently by a professional singer. Who he was and where he was remained mysteries but, as the German bombers were wholly absent that night, we lay in the darkness and enjoyed the impromptu bedtime concert. At the same time my mind was niggled by the incongruity of being entertained by someone who was presumably an enemy national, while those stark evidences of recent death and destruction were scattered over the Plain of Catania, only a few miles away.

We had stopped that night on the high ground immediately to the south of Aci Castello, and next morning it was announced that the Commando would be remaining in that area for the time being. We were marched to a narrow strip of land lying sandwiched between the coastal road and the sea, which was to be our new home. The cultivation terraces, cut into the steep hillside below the road, supported what seemed to be a haphazard mixture of almond trees, citrus fruits and vines. These ended with a rough, almost vertical drop of perhaps fifty feet down to the rocky coastline. We realized that this was the general area of the landing that had been proposed for us some three weeks earlier, and breathed belated sighs of relief. The thought of being dumped at the bottom of such cliffs, in the middle of the night, perhaps with a few hundred Germans in a rest area on the terraces above, made us doubly thankful that, in our turn, we had been put there just to 'rest'. We found it difficult enough to negotiate a way down to the sea for our daily swim. Moving in was a simple procedure, involving no more than dropping our gear and scraping away the topsoil. As we were still without any kit, apart from that which we had carried ashore, our daytime garb continued to be night attire plus boots. The officers appeared to fare somewhat better, as they were allotted a villa overlooking the Mediterranean and had apparently made some social contacts with the local bigwigs. One of these was reputed to be a duke, or at least a count, who was able to visit the officers' mess on a gleaming Moto Guzzi motorbike which could often be seen parked against the hedge outside.

By this time our cooks had progressed to having a makeshift galley equipped with a trestle table as a serving-counter. When collecting breakfast each morning we would also pick up the daily ration of cigarettes, boiled sweets or a bar of chocolate, a packet of hardtack biscuits and three sheets of toilet paper, all of which had been neatly set out in individual piles. The table stood in a small clearing on one of the upper terraces and, approaching from the shade of the trees, it looked precisely as you would imagine a film set for some South Seas castaway production, brilliantly illuminated by the Italian sun – just waiting for the director's call for 'Action! Camera!'

Our stay there passed pleasantly enough. Mornings were fully occupied with parades, rather low-key affairs in the circumstances, weapons inspections, fatigues, physical training and route marches. Afternoons were usually allocated to 'make do and mend' – the naval term for leaving you to your own devices with a view to darning socks, washing and repairing clothes, cleaning and polishing equipment etc, although in our reduced circumstances we could do very little along those lines.

The high point of each day was when we were able to disport ourselves in the Mediterranean. For most of us, then in our early twenties, who had been teenagers when the war started, this 'Italian holiday' type of enjoyment was something which we had never previously experienced and could scarcely have imagined for ourselves, even as a faint possibility. And, unlike Brúcoli, where there had been a two-mile walk in each direction, this was right on the doorstep, almost as if the Mediterranean was our own private swimming-pool. We cavorted in the water like porpoises, diving under one another and seeing who could stay under water the longest. We devised a game which we called 'O Group'. This, in the then current military jargon, was short for 'Order Group', the call sent around a unit when the commanding officer wished to gather his officers together to issue instructions. For us it was simply a matter of trying to meet up under water, at some predetermined rendezvous, with two or three others, all of whom had started off from different points along the rocky foreshore. If nothing else, it gave some interest to our swimming, and it was also probably very good for the lungs.

The local fishermen appeared to be more gainfully employed. They worked in pairs from a small rowing-boat with one man propelling it slowly over the placid sea while the other peered down into the water through a glass-bottomed bucket. We never learned just what it was that they were looking for but it gave the impression of being a pleasant and tranquil occupation – especially as we never saw them actually catch anything.

We were permitted a couple of afternoon 'trips ashore', to Acireale, the next town up the coast, but found that it had had very little to offer. The current best buy was 'limonada' – sugar, water and fresh lemon juice, made while you waited. It was an effective way of disguising the taste of the local water and also gave us a little practice at spending some of our Invasion Lire, but on the whole Acireale hadn't any great attraction.

A very welcome find, not far from the bivouac area, was

a clump of fig trees, flourishing amongst the ruins of a long-deserted building. It was in an overgrown spot, quite close to the usual route down to the sea, seemingly abandoned and forgotten about, but the fruit was deliciously ripe. The place was sufficiently hidden to remain unknown to all except those few who had come across it. We selfishly maintained strict secrecy about its existence, so were able to enjoy a session of fig-eating on the return from our swims. The main terraces were not neglected, however. Twice during our residence we were warned to 'Stand by your holes' because the Italians were going to irrigate. This, like the fishing in the bay, appeared to be a peaceful, interesting and unstrenuous occupation – breaking down little banks of earth to allow the water to flow where required, then cutting off the supply with a shovelful of soil when that particular area had received its ration. But a few good sleeping-spots were made uninhabitable for a day or two.

By 17 August the whole of Sicily was in Allied hands, and from about that time our life became more purposeful and our training sessions soon assumed a regular set pattern, the usual harbinger of an operation which had already been assigned to us. We found ourselves having to strike inland for a few miles, generally keeping away from the roads and seeming to make a point of slogging up any particularly steep and arduous hills we encountered *en route*. Once at the top of one of them, we would take up defensive positions, stay there for variable periods of time, then return to our bivouac area by a different route. At times we had to make a night of it. Leaving camp in the afternoon, we would do our approach march to the selected hill and, after climbing to the top, be allocated firing-positions and duty watches for periods of guard during the night. We would also often have some kind of dummy patrol to carry out.

There were three basic types of patrol – standing, recce ('recky' – reconnaissance) and fighting. Standing patrols, usually of an NCO and two men, would go forward of a position at various points, where they would conceal themselves and just wait and watch – to give advance warning of any approaching enemy. During the hours of darkness, when the ears were of more use than the eyes, they were generally referred to as 'night listening patrols'. The recce patrol – the kind we had carried out during the first two nights of the invasion – was a more active affair with the object of gaining information about the enemy's whereabouts (or his absence), preferably without drawing attention to yourselves. The fighting patrol was definitely intended to be aggressive and was usually much larger than either of the others, perhaps twenty men or more. It would probe forward into the enemy positions with the intention of causing disruption, creating alarm, inflicting casualties and, if possible – or this might even be the prime reason – bringing back a prisoner for interrogation, or just to discover which particular enemy formation was in action on that sector of the front.

After such a night exercise on some Italian hill, we would eat a makeshift breakfast, then wend our way back down to Aci Castello for the normal daytime routine. On one such occasion, as we tramped back along the coast road towards our bivouac area, the column was passed by a large, open-topped staff car heading in the opposite direction – north, towards Messina. Anything that might take your mind off a monotonous march was always worthy of scrutiny. This time we saw a black beret sporting two cap badges and realized that this was our commander in chief, General Montgomery. We guessed that he probably didn't have any idea who we were.

It was eventually admitted that a particular sea-borne landing had been planned for us, and it wasn't too difficult to guess that it would be on the mainland of Italy. What we hadn't expected to hear was that some men of the Fighting Troops were likely to be left behind in Sicily along with the rear echelon and the sick. For some reason it had been decided that a slimmed-down Commando was to be used. By this time most of us had grown rather bored with our passive role since the Sicily landing and were eager to start earning our keep again. For some days we lived in dread of being singled out to stay behind, so it was an unqualified relief to learn that Q Troop would be going *en bloc*, the only exceptions being those who were actually on the sick list. On a personal level, on this occasion I would stick to my Lee Enfield rifle. We were also told that, although No. 40 Commando would be staying with the British Eighth Army, our own involvement with it would soon be at an end.

For the coming operation, 41 Commando would be linked with No. 2 Army Commando to form a British Commando Brigade to be attached to the American Fifth Army under US General Mark Clark. The Fifth Army was a recently created formation and, despite its name and the nationality of its Commander, about fifty per cent of its troops were British, including the 46th and 56th Divisions. We also learned that, in addition to the British Commandos, three battalions of Rangers,* the American equivalent, would also be taking part. They were under the command of Colonel Bill Darby. Their 1st Battalion of about 500 men had been formed from 2,000 who responded to a call for volunteers made to the US Forces in Northern Ireland in May 1942. These men constituted the first Ranger course at the Commando Training Centre at Achnacarry and so had a close link with the British Commandos. The 1st Battalion had been the nucleus for the formation of all three Ranger battalions involved in the Salerno operation. Having earned their coveted green berets, most of the original members of the 1st Battalion continued to wear them throughout their subsequent service life, even when posted to other units.

It was on the last day of August that General Clark sent a string of American TCVs (Troop-Carrying Vehicles) to collect us. They arrived in the late evening and were unobtrusively lined up on the road above our bivouac area. We immediately loaded them with the ammunition and other stores that were to be taken along, in readiness for the early start scheduled for the following morning.

Only minutes after we had settled down for the night, our ears picked up the drone of approaching aircraft. This

---

* The name was derived from Roger's Rangers, a troop of Indian fighters at the time of the New England Colonies in the mid-eighteenth century, rather than the Texas Rangers, as is sometimes assumed.

was unusual in the extreme, as there had been no air activity in our neighbourhood for the past weeks. The sound increased until the planes – there seemed to be about six of them – were directly overhead. Then the hairs on the back of our necks stood to attention as the whole area was bathed in the glaring white light of a batch of parachute flares.

Any thoughts that this was nothing more than a chance visit were soon dispelled. The engine noises changed from a low drone to a purposeful roar and then up to a high-pitched scream, as the planes took it in turn to dive low, strafing the area with machine-gun and cannon fire. The flares floated slowly downwards, swinging gently to and fro beneath their little canopies, keeping the whole countryside brightly illuminated. For perhaps twenty minutes the aircraft kept it up with complete impunity, dropping more flares as required and roaring down with guns and cannon blazing, time and time again. There was absolutely no answering fire from the ground, nor did any of our planes try to interfere. If this was a ploy to make the attackers believe that there was nothing worthwhile beneath their flares, it may have succeeded. The attack eventually fizzled out and, so far as we were aware, nothing was lost apart from some badly wanted sleep.

We embussed at four o'clock in the morning, and the convoy moved off without delay, heading south towards Catania. The massive trucks maintained a good speed, and in a matter of minutes we were trundling through the outskirts of the still slumbering city, then out into the open countryside, jolting and slithering along a rough road which wound its way through the foothills of Mount Etna. We were heading for Palermo, on the northern coast of the island, not much more than 120 miles away as the crow flies. But it soon became apparent – from the rough state of the roads and the great number of demolished bridges *en route* – that the journey would be much more protracted than the flight of any crow.

Certainly no charge of dawdling could be levelled against our drivers. They were Negroes to a man, and all seemed imbued with the single burning desire of getting us (or was it, perhaps, themselves?) across that island in the shortest possible time. On roads that were little more than narrow mountain tracks hugging the edge of a nothingness which threatened a sheer drop into eternity, those Yanks slithered their huge trucks around blind bends with an abandon that made our toenails curl. Inside the TCVs we swayed and bounced about on the hard, slatted seats, hanging on for grim death – but ready, at a moment's notice, to jump for our lives.

Down on the plain the roads were wider and without those awesome drops at the side, so it was possible to breathe a little more freely and take stock of the countryside through which we were passing. It was a parched and barren scrubland, seemingly lifeless and completely deserted – as flat as the proverbial pancake, except that, here and there, the wide plain was relieved by the towering, truncated cones of isolated, imposing hills. Our route took us close enough to some of these to see that, at the very top of almost every one, looking rather like the capping of an Egyptian pyramid, was perched a compact and seemingly inaccessible little town.

But even in the lowlands it wasn't possible to relax completely. Every bridge had been demolished by the retreating Germans, and American sappers had formed alternative crossings by constructing rough roadways down the banks of the almost dry rivers. Our drivers tackled these diversions with gusto. The trucks would career down the steep bankside, bounce frighteningly over the rock-covered river bed, then roar unsteadily up the other side. The engine, racing madly at first and seemingly able to take everything in its stride as it was clashed down through the gears, would eventually begin to labour as the truck neared the top of the further bank. With no more gears left and turning more and more slowly, it was touch and go whether it would stall before finally dragging us onto the road at the other side. After each successful sally, we breathed a grateful sigh of relief. But all drivers weren't so good – or perhaps so lucky – as ours. We passed two of the TCVs keeled over on their sides, having spilled their passengers out onto the roadside – luckily with nothing more than a few bruises. Notwithstanding the very early start, it had long been dark by the time we dropped, stiffly but thankfully, from the backs of our TCVs onto *terra firma* again. The Commando had been deposited at the entrance of a field bordered by a small wood. A bivouac area was already prepared for us: mosquito nets were in position, and there were fire trenches, a piped water supply and American Negro sentries. We were all in one piece, Mark Clark had fixed us up with a camp and given us packets of 'Lucky Strike' cigarettes, and there would be no guard duty that night. So when we crawled under the mosquito nets with our bellies filled with unaccustomed foods, it was enough to be going on with.

Next morning we could see that we had been transported to a more agricultural than vinicultural part of Sicily. The bivouac area, we discovered, was close to the village of Misilmeri, lying some eight miles south of the island's major port and naval base of Palermo.

That day lives in memory as the one on which we really appreciated that, being attached to an American Army, we would actually receive American food. Five-man packs of active service rations are probably not everyone's idea of *haute cuisine* but, after weeks of British compo, we thought they were from another world. Compared with compo tea, the American coffee was nectar, and the completely new tastes of fruit juice and sweetcorn were like living at the Ritz. The candy ration was much more generous than ours: the rolls of lifebelt-shaped, fruity acid drops called 'Lifesavers', in particular, were eminently suckable in that thirsty climate, and there was – as if we could have doubted it – chewing-gum. On top of all that, the American biscuits weren't quite so hard as the British variety and even tasted better. We were also intrigued by the instructions on the ration boxes, setting out the recommended procedure for utilizing the food-packaging materials to make a fire.

But we weren't there just for a change of diet. Training marches became a daily routine, and very soon we were feeling that, if not the mad dogs, we certainly were the

Englishmen (together with our kindred Scotsmen, Irishmen and Welshmen) who went out in the midday sun, particularly when our sweating, tramping column was smothered in the dust and high-spirited banter of a bunch of truck-borne Yanks – who never seemed to march anywhere.

Three days after our arrival at Misilmeri (on 3 September), the Eighth Army moved across the Straits of Messina to land on the toe of mainland Italy. No. 40 Commando helped things along by going ashore at Vibo Valentia. It was also memorable to us, in a very minor sort of way, as the day the Americans laid on transport for an afternoon trip to Palermo. The city streets were thronged with promenading American military personnel, all spick and span in clean, well-pressed uniforms and polished boots. In our distinctly grubby and exceedingly crumpled KSDs, the British were, without any doubt at all, the country cousins. After locating the post office, a monumental Mussolini-inspired, mock-Doric edifice, to purchase some postage stamps as souvenirs, we were directed to a highly efficient soda-fountain. Unexpectedly, we found it to be precisely like those we had seen on the movies, even to having smartly uniformed American girls behind the counters. Apart from the girls, who were strictly 'GI' (Government Issue) and probably only for Americans, we found little sufficiently gripping for us to want to go back to the big city.

At Misilmeri we were still sleeping '*al giorno*' – dressed as in daytime – in the same one and only khaki drill uniform, with no more than a mosquito net over our heads. The nights were wholly peaceful, with no suggestion of enemy aircraft. On only one occasion did we have a rude awakening, and that was to find ourselves wet and uncomfortable under the first rainfall we had experienced since leaving Scotland. After two hours of uncomfortable huddling together under the dubious protection of mosquito nets and the overhanging branches of trees, the shower ended soon after daybreak and the hot sun rapidly dried us out.

On 7 September, four days after our first visit, we had a

second trip to Palermo, but it was only to use the port facilities. Early in the afternoon, armed, accoutred and accompanied by our ammunition and stores, we climbed on board another line of General Clark's TCVs and in no time at all were jolting through the city. The imminent departure of the American Fifth Army had made no noticeable impression upon the multitudes of well-scrubbed Americans parading the streets. For our part, despite previous opinions and comments on the place, and about getting back to work, it looked very attractive this time, and we would probably have opted to stay for a while if we had been asked – but we weren't.

Our string of TCVs continued towards the docks and was soon worming its way through droves of fully armed troops, some in trucks but most on foot, all heading for their assigned embarkation points. When we came within sight of the Mediterranean, we could hardly see the water for ships, of more different types than we could put names to. Closer at hand were the ones which were our direct concern, scores of LCI(S)s – Landing-Craft Infantry (Small), moored bows-in to the quays and giving a purposeful edging to all the bustling activity in the docks area. Trucks were off-loading men and materials in a continuous flood, while long crocodiles of heavily burdened infantrymen were filing aboard their craft. Other lines of troops in working dress, who would probably be drinking beer in the Palermo pubs afterwards, were passing boxes of ammunition, food and stores hand to hand from dockside to deck of ship after ship after ship.

Our TCVs came to a stop directly in front of the craft to which we had been assigned. We debussed and trooped on board to be quickly followed by the stores which were to accompany us. No sooner was everything on the deck than our LCI eased away from the quay to make room for another one.

LCI(S)s accommodated up to a hundred men, housed in three small mess decks, which were little more than steel boxes with attached washroom and toilets. The distinctive features of these vessels was the pair of landing-ramps lying exposed on the foredeck ready to be launched over the bows, when the craft had been embedded on a beach. Our craft steamed slowly out into the wide expanse of the outer harbour where it dropped anchor to await the completion of the embarkation procedure involving the tens of thousands of men who had been chosen to carry out that particular mission. Even before the assemblage of the whole task force had been completed, the sea was dotted with a staggering number of vessels, score upon score, seemingly without end. It was comforting to see that there were a great number of LCIs, just like ours – the chaps at the sharp end. We sat in the warm sunshine, writing the customary last letters, again using stubs of pencils and sheets of notepaper provided by our Royal Navy hosts. As we wrote, our eyes were continually straying to the movements of the multitude of ships all around. What, we wondered, was in store for us this time?

Daylight was almost gone and the outlines of the more distant vessels had become blurred and indistinct when the engines throbbed into life. Anchors were winched aboard and our LCI slipped into its place amongst that host of vessels all heading for the open sea, *en route* for – somewhere in Italy.

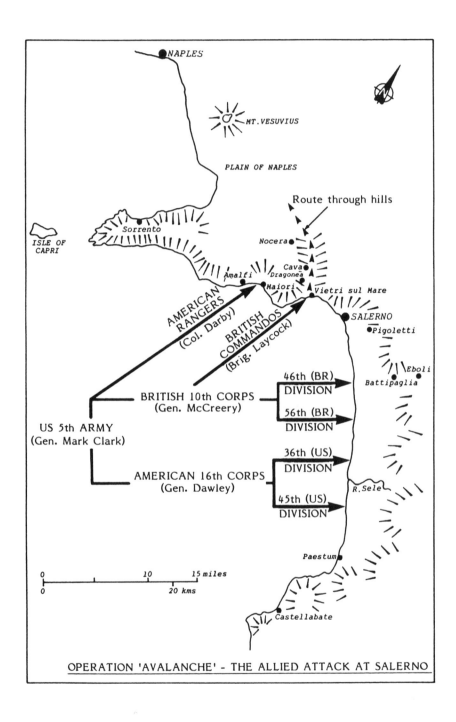

OPERATION 'AVALANCHE' - THE ALLIED ATTACK AT SALERNO

8 *The Salerno Landing*

On the morning of 8 September we awoke to a brilliant sky and a shimmering sea. Once again it was to marvel at the sight of a vast armada of ships and landing-craft of all sizes and types, widely spaced out over a placid ocean. They appeared to cover the entire surface, stretching from horizon to horizon and to every point of the compass. This huge fleet was forging ahead almost sedately, certainly without any suggestion of haste, and by its very immensity seemed to exude an aura of relentless purpose. Our first reaction was to wonder how such a vast assemblage of vessels could possibly escape detection from a watchful enemy.

On board the landing-craft the morning was spent in cleaning and oiling weapons, yet again, and making any necessary final checks and adjustments to webbing equipment. In the afternoon we were called together to be briefed on the forthcoming operation. There was now no security risk in telling us that the destination of the Fifth Army was the Bay of Salerno, with the main purpose of the landing being the capture of the port of Naples, lying some thirty miles to the north of the town. The British Eighth Army, which had landed on the toe of Italy five days previously, was pushing its way up the leg of the country, but every item of equipment and supply was having to be landed over open beaches, a difficult, manpower- and time-consuming business. If the momentum of the Allies' drive towards Rome was not to peter out, a major port was required as soon as possible. As a secondary benefit, a landing in force behind the German lines would create a diversion, probably forcing them to withdraw troops from the south and take some pressure off the Eighth Army. Unlike the Sicily operation, the air support which could be provided on this occasion would be minimal, as the nearest Sicilian airfields were almost at the limit of the operational range of Allied fighter aircraft.

The chosen beaches extend for about twenty-five miles southwards from the town of Salerno. They are the only ones on that stretch of the Italian coast which are suitable to accommodate the immense and complicated procedures involved in landing an army which could build up to well over 100,000 men, with all their tanks, guns, trucks, munitions and stores. The landing-zone was roughly bisected by the River Sele, and although the Fifth Army was a unified Allied force under a single commander, the initial assault had been planned as two separate thrusts, with the British divisions going ashore to the north of the Sele and the Americans to the south. A major drawback of the chosen area, from a military standpoint, was that the flat coastal strip is hemmed in by lofty hills rising to some 3,500 feet, which greatly restricts the area of countryside available for the deployment of a large military force.

The intended direction of the Allied advance was, clearly, to be northwards – towards the Plain of Naples, and the only practicable route through the hills was that used by the main road and railway line which wind their way through two narrow passes lying to the north of Salerno. It was to be the task of the British Commando brigade and the American Ranger battalions to go ashore independently and well to the north of the main landing-beaches, occupy the heights commanding these two defiles and ensure that they were kept open for the passage of the Fifth Army, who might otherwise be bottled up in their beachhead. In addition to keeping the road open for the advancing Fifth Army, command of these two routes through the hills would prevent their being used by the Germans in reinforcing their troops facing the Fifth Army landings. The first of the passes is called 'La Molina', often referred to as 'the Cave Defile' as it carries the road and railway from Vietri sul Mare, a seaside town about two miles north of Salerno, inland towards the small town of Cava. Holding this was to be the task of the British Commandos. Thereafter the route to Naples continues in the direction of the town of Nocera via the 'Nocera Defile', and the job of safeguarding that part of the route had been given to the US Rangers.

The British Commando Brigade had been code-named 'Layforce' as it was under the overall command of Brigadier Bob Laycock, who later that year was to take over from Lord Louis Mountbatten as Chief of Combined Operations. It was to be landed at Marina de Vietri, the beach of the coastal town of Vietri sul Mare. No. 2 Commando would go ashore first to establish a beachhead, then they would secure the left flank of No. 41, who were to pass through them, and swing to the right a short distance down the coast to capture Vietri. When that had been accomplished, both Commandos would go up into the hills to secure the Molina pass and hold it until the Fifth Army had pushed its forward units up to them and taken over. (We immediately recognized the pattern of our training exercises at Aci Castello.) After keeping the defile open until the Fifth Army had relieved us (which we were assured would be only a matter of hours, twenty-four at the most), our job would be finished and we would move back to the beachhead. This was something new for Royal Marines, who generally get the reputation for being 'first in – last out'. We considered this new proposal, of 'first in – first out', a much more logical idea.

The American Ranger battalions were to go ashore about seven miles to our left, further along the coast of the Sorrento peninsula, near the town of Maiori on the road to Amalfi, then strike inland to seize the Nocera Defile.

Briefing for our personal involvement in the operation was sketchy in the extreme. In essence it was no more than, 'Follow the man in front, do what you are told, and once you have dug in on the top of your hill, STAY THERE.' Not a lot to memorize. We were dismissed and lay down on the deck in the sun to mull over what we had been told. It struck us as being something of a coincidence to be on our way to take part in the capture of the home town of the men of the Napoli Division, who had been opposing us in Sicily. We also seemed to have some sort of an affinity with volcanoes – having recently bidden farewell to Mount Etna, we were going to be put ashore within a score of miles of Mount Vesuvius.

In the late afternoon, with ammunition issued and grenades primed, without incident this time, we were sitting around, still talking things over as there was little else to do, when a single enemy plane put in a bombing attack on the convoy at some distance ahead of us. A barrage of guns peppered the sky with white puffs of shellbursts, and streams of tracers could be seen arcing their way upwards, then vicious spouts of water showed where the bombs were falling. It was all over in a matter of minutes, and neither ships nor plane appeared to have suffered any damage. Our main concern then was that, as the invasion fleet had obviously been spotted, it was probably only a matter of time before a massive enemy reaction would be visited upon us. Anxious eyes scanned the sky in all directions, and ears were cocked for the first tell-tale sound of aero-engines. We watched and waited, and waited and watched until, to our uncomprehending relief, the fading daylight gave way to a deepening dusk without any further incident. Despite our experience in Augusta harbour, we still felt that there would be greater safety under the cloak of darkness.

There were to be no more attacks by enemy bombers but, before the dusk had deepened into full darkness, a veritable bombshell of news was dropped amongst us. We were told that General Eisenhower had, that very evening, announced the unconditional surrender of the Italian Government and that Mussolini was in captivity. For a few short moments we imagined that our part in that particular theatre of war would now be over, and mad conjectures buzzed around in our heads. Perhaps the convoy would turn around and sail back to Sicily, or maybe we would carry on to steam openly into Naples harbour next morning and troop down the landing-ramps in full daylight, to the cheers of the populace. Such ideas were quickly dispelled. We were reminded that there were still very many Germans in Italy who were not likely to be swayed by this action of their reluctant allies. The landing would go ahead as planned – the only difference being that there was now no doubt that we would be facing German rather than Italian troops.

By this time the more distant vessels of the task force had been swallowed up in the darkness. As our range of vision progressively shortened, we became more and more alone. From the sparse information filtering down to us, it appeared that during the day the invasion fleet had passed Salerno, steaming northwards, roughly parallel to the Italian coast, in an endeavour to keep the Germans in some doubt as to the actual point of attack. Now, under the cover of darkness, the various elements of the force had turned around and were heading for their respective landing-beaches. The craft carrying the Commando Brigade had sailed well beyond Vietri sul Mare, out into the Bay of Naples, and were back-tracking down the coast towards our own little beach.

At one point we were told that only a few miles away to port, although completely invisible in the velvet blackness of the night, lay the Isle of Capri. The lyrics of a popular pre-war song insinuated themselves into my brain:

'Twas on the Isle of Capri that I found her,
Beneath the shade of an old walnut tree –
I can still see the flowers blooming round her,
When we met on the Isle of Capri …

It must have been just about the same time of the year too:

Summertime was nearly over,
Blue Italian skies above …

Well, I supposed, we would see about that part of it in the morning.

It was a moonless night, and the skyline of Italy was barely distinguishable as our flotilla of landing-craft nosed slowly in towards the shore. Any last lingering thoughts that our part in the Italian war might have come to an end were soon dispelled. To the north, long fingers of searchlights began probing the dark sky, seeking out the Allied bombers which would be flying in to carry out their diversionary attack in the area of Naples. Almost immediately, the sporadic flashes of bursting bombs began to present us with a sharp silhouette of the tops of the intervening hills. Somewhere in the black nothingness below those peaks, the American Rangers would also be approaching their landfall.

Away to the south, from the direction of the Fifth Army's main landing-beaches, we heard a dull rumble of gunfire which told us that things were getting off to a noisy start down there. But our sector of the coast remained absolutely quiet and undisturbed. Engines were throttled back, and the indistinct shapes of the other craft could just be made out, in line abreast on both sides of us as they edged in towards the featureless black mass ahead. Crew members were crouching low in the bows, ready to launch the landing-ramps. We were ranged along each side of the deckhouse, down on one knee, weapons at the ready, eyes straining to pierce the darkness.

The beach became vaguely discernible as nothing more than a slightly lighter patch in the obscurity ahead; engines were stopped and the slow headway of the craft became completely silent. Were the Jerries waiting to see the whites of our eyes or had they really packed up and gone home? With only a slight judder, the bows grounded, the ramps were heaved forward and, even as we heard the dull thumps of them striking the damp sand, some fifteen feet below, we were running – along the deck, then down the wooden slope and onto the firm sand. A dry landing! Good old Navy! In seconds we were rushing across a flat, deserted beach towards the black shapes of tall buildings which could just be distinguished, appearing to rise from the very sand itself.

The beach ended at a low sea wall barely two feet high, which we cleared in a single stride that carried us onto a smooth paved surface. In that fleeting fraction of a second between beach and roadway, I glimpsed a sandbagged machine-gun position, down on the sand, backed against the sea wall but completely deserted. Breathing a quick prayer of thankfulness, we continued to race forward, our rubber-soled boots making scarcely a sound, until we darted into the welcoming blackness of a narrow alleyway leading from the seafront. There we paused briefly to catch up with our breathing and get organized.

As soon as the section had assembled, we moved off again, padding along silently behind Lieutenant Haydon and Corporal Maley (acting as section sergeant, in the absence of Sergeant Shepherd, left behind in Sicily with blood-poisoning). We hastened along narrow streets that were no more than footways squeezed between the towering black walls of the flanking buildings. We were making no noise, but a curious fantasia of 'plipping' and 'plopping' filled the darkness around us. Then we realized what the source of the puzzling noises was – dripping water-taps! The taps were fixed to the walls of the buildings, and each household must have had one of their own. With every few paces we passed another, and they all seemed to need their washers attended to. Running past them it was curious to hear that every tap had its own individual drip pattern. There were 'plop, plop, plops', 'plup, plip, pleps', rapid-fire 'plip,plip,plip,plip,plips' and occasionally some deep, resounding 'ploooomp, ploooomps', where extra-large drops were falling into a water-filled trough. We passed through Marina with our movements lost in the shadows and the faint scufflings of our feet masked by a medley of dripping water-taps.

After only a few more minutes we began to ascend a flight of stone steps. Then another – and another – and another. We soon left the black bowl of Marina behind and moved out into the semi-darkness of the open sky. The steps continued upwards, flight after flight, until we were wondering whether they would ever end. With leg muscles aching and chests heaving as we gasped for breath, we had to struggle madly to keep up with the man in front. After what seemed to be an age, there were, thank goodness, no more steps; we lurched forward onto the flat white carriageway of the coastal road.

Leg muscles welcomed the change but, without any pause, had to carry us on at a steady run. We crossed the road obliquely to our right, moving rapidly forward in the direction of Vietri. It was much lighter here, and even in the semi-darkness we could see our way quite clearly along the light-coloured surface of the road which, after only a few hundred yards, led us out onto a high, exposed viaduct. Still running at the double, we bent our heads low to present as small a target as possible and kept widely spaced out to reduce the effect of any burst of fire, should the enemy be waiting for us in the inky blackness on the other side. The roadway was littered with shell splinters as though it had recently been on the receiving end of a softening-up shoot by the Navy. Our hurrying feet sent the jagged slivers of steel tinkling over the hard surface. Reaching the other side safely, we were relieved to be swallowed up in a tunnel of blackness at the left-hand side of the road, formed over a steeply sloping footpath which led us upwards between a high retaining wall and a row of trees flanking the carriageway.

It was barely possible to make out the shadowy shape of the man in front as we ran through the darkness, so that when, suddenly, the leaders stopped, everyone concertina-ed to a halt with an involuntary mutter of hushed curses. I was third or fourth man down the line and heard Corporal Maley's hoarse whisper of 'Machine-gun!' This was immediately followed by a *sotto voce* decision to use a hand-grenade rather than a tommy-gun. Then followed the faint noises of a grenade being unclipped and thrown. At that instant the gun's crew must have realized what was happening. Perhaps before the grenade hit the ground, certainly before it exploded, we heard a mad scatter of heavy boots on the roadway. Immediately after the detonation, we rushed forward, brushing past the muzzle of the abandoned machine-gun trained directly down the line of our approach and hardly a dozen yards from the place where we had stopped. Of the machine-gunners there was no sign. We chased around trying to find them but they had melted into the empty and silent streets of Vietri.

At this point Q Troop was split in two. No. 8 section filed away down a street to the left, with the job of straddling the main road and disrupting any traffic they might find there. No. 7 carried on into the centre of the town to occupy the main crossroads and take up defensive positions to hold it against a possible counter-attack. As we were still moving forward, the silence was broken by the unmistakable sounds of a long burst of bren fire and an irregular volley of rifle shots coming from the direction of the main road; then all was quiet again.

Reaching the crossroads, Corporal Maley began allocating firing-positions: 'Bren group – there; riflemen – there, there and there.' When it came to my turn, his roving eye, assessing the military possibilities of the position, spotted a first-floor balcony on a building at one corner of the crossroads. 'Right, Mitch,' he whispered. 'You can be look-out – up there and keep your eyes skinned.' There was a convenient drainpipe running down the corner formed by the balcony and the main wall of the building, so the climb wasn't difficult. But when I reached up, grasped the metal balustrade and tried to haul myself over, I found it impossible to move – something in the region of the small of my back held me fast. Trying to ease downwards didn't help either; it was clear that some part of my equipment had become snarled up on a wire spanning between building and balcony. I could move neither up nor down and for a few agonizing moments sweated helplessly on the drainpipe. At last, presumably with the strength of desperation, I made another frantic heave upwards and shot over the railings, while my gas mask, torn from its securing brasses on the back of my belt, plopped onto the pavement below.

My look-out position was not very extensive – about eight feet long by four wide, with a louvred timber door set in the wall of the building. There were faint sounds of movement from the other side of the door, so, when I had recovered my breath, with rifle at the ready, I tried the handle, only to find it locked. Reporting the situation to Lieutenant Haydon in the street below, I was told to forget the noises and just keep my eyes open for Germans. The balcony was equipped with little more than a small sink and a tap – which, surprisingly, I thought, didn't drip – plus an old wooden chair. I settled down on the chair, rifle at the ready across my knees to wait and watch in some comfort. The interior of the building went quiet, and the whole of Vietri too seemed to slip back into slumber and silence. Only a continuous sullen rumble of gunfire from the main Salerno landing-beaches disturbed our warm Italian night. Hanging from hooks above the sink were a few bunches of grapes, so I was able to enjoy some of the fruits of war during the remaining uneventful hour or two of darkness.

As the sky lightened with the dawn, Vietri started to show signs of coming to life. More indistinguishable noises from within the room brought my rifle round in that direction. I heard the bolts being carefully drawn and watched the door open ever so slowly and cautiously until the gap was wide enough to reveal a rather apprehensive face. It was a man, small, middle-aged and definitely civilian, dressed in nightclothes and dressing-gown. He was holding a jug in his hand and motioned, questioningly, towards the water-tap. When I nodded a magnanimous, 'OK', his face relaxed into a broad smile as he bustled forward. Before filling the jug, he took down a bunch of grapes, which he washed carefully under the tap, then put them on a plate which he proffered me with a friendly 'Help yourself!' gesture. Feeling rather guilty about having already eaten a goodly portion of his stock – and unwashed too – but not wishing to hurt his feelings, I graciously accepted with a 'Grazie' and popped one or two into my mouth while he was drawing his water. We attempted no further conversation for, apart from the language barrier, it is difficult to imagine what kind of small-talk could pass between an unsuspecting civilian and an invading enemy soldier who had materialized on his balcony in the middle of the night. As he re-entered the room, I caught sight of an equally middle-aged lady awaiting his return with obvious trepidation.

A few curious Italians now began to show themselves in the streets below me, first in ones and twos, then more and more, until Lieutenant Haydon and Corporal Maley, with the help of some Italians who could have been local officials, began directing them back towards Marina for their own safety. A cheerful, market-day, 'Come and see the Tommies' situation now ensued, and there seemed to be no doubt that the residents of Vietri sul Mare looked upon their British invaders as *'amici'*. Possibly, too, they were impressed by our prompt arrival – less than twelve hours after their Government had surrendered. Nevertheless, the marines continued to maintain vigilance in their firing-positions and left the public-relations side to the officer and corporal. Driblets of information began to filter through, and I found myself in a useful position for eavesdropping when Lieutenant Haydon received any messages.

It was confirmed that the small-arms fire heard shortly after No. 8 Section left us had been their doing. Scarcely were they positioned to command the highway than a German half-track, towing a 105mm gun, came trundling round a bend heading for Salerno. Simmo (L/Cpl. Simpson), on the bren, and the riflemen of the section had opened fire, killing the driver and other occupants of the front seat. The vehicle careered off the road, spilling out the other dozen or so sleepy Germans who, bruised and bemused, were taken prisoner before they knew what had happened. Not until much later did I learn that there had also been a scout car accompanying the half-track. This had entered Vietri with an officer standing up in the front seat blazing away with his Luger automatic, Wild West style, until disposed of by our Troop sniper, Harry Weiss.

By now the sun had dispelled the shadows of the night, and from my vantage-point I had a wide view over the pantiled roofs of part of the town and out to the steep, tree-clad hills beyond. It was a pleasant, peaceful scene until the quiet was disturbed by the unmistakable multiple whine of an approaching salvo of shells or mortar bombs. Seconds later came the 'crummmp-crummmp-crummmp-crummmps' of their arrival. I saw spurts of smoke and debris rise where the shells had fallen upon the houses only a few hundred yards in front of me. The street below cleared like magic. Smoke and dust were still billowing over the rooftops when a second salvo came in, followed by a third and a fourth. The shellbursts were moving closer and closer to the crossroads until they were falling less than a hundred yards away. It was disconcerting to be stuck between heaven and earth, like Juliet on her balcony, with nowhere to duck, hoping fervently that the next command to the German gunners would not be 'Up – 100!' – or whatever they said in the *Wehrmacht* – to increase the range. Fortunately my hopes were realized: the shells came no nearer, and after a few more salvoes the firing stopped altogether.

Whether or not the artillery fire had played any part in the decision is a matter of conjecture, but we were soon given orders to move out. 'All right, Mitch!' called Jan Maley. 'Come on down.' I decided to use the stairs this time and entered the room, motioning to my hosts that I was leaving. They smiled happily, the man hastened to open the door for me, and as I walked past, he patted my shoulder repeating, *'Buon soldato, buon soldato.'* It was rather flattering to be called a 'good soldier', but it was much more comforting to be able to return to ground-level, where there was at least some room for manœuvre.

We formed up in the street, now growing hot in the rising sun, and marched off – to the waves and smiles of the populace who had surfaced again as soon as the shelling stopped. We returned to Marina by a different route and were soon descending the flights of steps we had found so punishing on the way up. In daylight we could see that Marina was built up in tiers against the hillside like one half of a Roman amphitheatre. It seemed to be accessible only on foot – or perhaps, by donkey – and was a veritable Clovelly of Campania. Down and down we tramped, then back up the other side, without even seeing the beach. Sweating and panting, leg muscles aching once more, we emerged onto a white dusty road snaking its way ahead of us along the coast and up into the hills. It was probably the same road used during the night, so we couldn't understand the necessity of having to go back down into Marina, but ours was not to reason why. In any case there were other things to occupy our minds for, as our long file was trudging up the road, the bombardment of Vietri was resumed. It was clear that the Italian surrender had had no effect upon the German's intention of letting us know that we weren't welcome.

As the road climbed higher, we gained more impressive views of the Mediterranean, looking cool and eminently tempting some hundreds of feet below us, to our left. We passed very few Italians but they, unlike the people of Vietri, who had seemed reasonably pleased to see us, watched our march-past with expressionless faces. After a mile or so we reached a group of drab grey buildings which seemed to be the beginning of a village. The column ahead had moved across to the right-hand side of the road and was disappearing through a doorway set in a high stone wall. When we in our turn reached the opening and passed through, it was to take a step from the bright sunshine of the open road into the broken shade of a multitude of trees. We found ourselves on a narrow track of beaten earth leading steeply up a well-wooded hillside, and a few yards beyond the wall a considerable stockpile of ammunition for the heavy machine-guns had been accumulated. When we reached the heap of steel boxes, each containing 250 cartridges, every man was handed one to carry – 'just to the top'.

For about an hour after that we trudged higher and higher, first on the same slippery track through the trees, then following a rough and rocky farm road which led us eventually to the farm itself. Here we were relieved to be halted for a short 'stand easy'. Deployed as usual for all-round defence, I was fortunate to be given a position on a paved terrace overlooking the Mediterranean. We were now perhaps 2,000 feet above sea-level and had a magnificent view in the general direction of Amalfi, Sorrento and the Isle of Capri. Somewhere over there the American Rangers would be going about their part of the business, and we wondered how they were faring. Looking at the calm, sparkling sea far below, it was difficult to realize that only a few short hours previously we had been down there, slipping quietly through those waters in the dead of night. Well, so far, so good – and, as in the ballad, we certainly had those 'blue Italian skies above'.

Posted alongside me on the terrace was one of the Commando who had remained in the UK with the rear echelon and had only recently rejoined the unit in Sicily. I hadn't met him previously but soon found that we had at least one thing in common – the name Mitchell – no relation and I don't recall ever seeing him again. As we chatted in the sunshine, he made me feel a little like the Ancient Mariner when he said, in a voice tinged with envy, 'Of course, this is your *second* landing!' All too soon our rest period came to an end with the unfailing, 'All Right! Get fell in.'

It was mid afternoon before we finally reached the top of the hill and were able to drop those boxes of machine-gun ammunition. We plodded on for a further few hundred yards before being allocated our firing-positions. Then patrols were sent out, probing forward to see if there were any of the enemy already in occupation. They returned with 'Nil' reports.

The summit of the hill was shaped like an elongated oval with its nose pointing inland in the general direction of Cava. The long right-hand side, or front, of the hill overlooked La Molina pass. The terrain was rough grass with rock outcrops, well covered with trees, although these were in the main rather small and spindly. When we had been arranged into our defensive perimeter, it extended for perhaps 400 yards from nose to tail and about 150 yards from La Molina back to the rather indeterminate, tree-covered slope on the other side. Within this envelope the spine of the hill rose for a further forty or fifty feet into a tangle of rocks and bushes interspersed with areas of grass. Q Troop was strung out along part of the rear of the hill, away from La Molina, where the grass slope fell away steeply to lose itself in a sea of foliage only about thirty yards from our positions. Working in pairs, taking it in turns to keep a look-out and to wield an entrenching tool, we dug ourselves in. By evening we had excavated reasonable slit trenches. Night-listening patrols were posted forward of the position.

As usual we carried our own food for the first forty-eight hours of the operation, and this time it was two packs of 'K rations', the American one-man/one-day issue. Each ration was contained in a stiff waxed paper carton which wasn't nearly so heavy, or so bulky, as the motley collection of tin cans we had humped ashore on Sicily. For most of us the meat content for that day had long since been eaten, so our evening meal was reduced to cheese and biscuits washed down with tepid water from our bottles. Duty watches were set and, as darkness fell, the still silence enshrouding our hill only served to accentuate the noise of gunfire coming from the Salerno beachhead, a continuous rolling grumble in the distance.

It was obvious that the main force hadn't made much progress in our direction and, although we had no definite knowledge of the situation, it was already apparent that we could not expect to see them quite as soon as had been anticipated. It was also rumoured that the Germans had received intelligence of the time and place of the main assault and so had concentrated their available forces to meet it. This would have explained the empty machine-gun positions on the beach at Marina and our unopposed landing, but we had no way of knowing the facts. Certainly the enemy hadn't anticipated a Commando landing to secure La Molina, so we had that much to be thankful for.

There seemed little doubt that the troops down on the Salerno beaches were having a pretty rough time of it, but for us up on our hill that night under the stars passed quietly and without incident. We alternated between periods of eye-straining watchfulness and the dreamless sleep of the weary.

9   *Holding the Road to Naples*

Next morning, when the Commando was stood to in readiness to meet any dawn attack, it was still dark. Crouching in our foxholes, we watched and waited in complete silence, weapons nestling in our hands. No movement or talking was permitted. The minutes passed by with exasperating slowness, and many times, as in Sicily, you would debate with yourself whether or not there really had been a movement down there in the blackness below you, or whether it was no more than your imagination. Then, time and again, you would occupy your mind in trying to decide whether the hillside to your front was perhaps not quite so dark as it had been.

After what seemed an age, the time did arrive when you were in no doubt that the night sky had become a shade or so lighter. If there was to be a dawn attack, this was just about the time for it. However, even when the sky had become noticeably brighter, it was only the chirruping of the awakening birds that broke the silence. Eventually the slowly rising sun had eased the last lingerings of night from under the trees, but still we waited, motionless. It was full daylight and there was a welcome warmth in the sun before we were at last allowed to stand down, breathe freely, stretch stiff and cramped limbs and talk.

Standing patrols were immediately posted forward of the Commando position to give advance warning of any approaching enemy, while the rest of us turned our thoughts towards breakfast. Chins were bristly on this our second morning ashore but there was little enough water left in our bottles to wash down the American biscuits for breakfast, let alone contemplate having a shave. Water had become top priority, and arrangements had to be made to replenish stocks as soon as possible. We were told that somewhere down the back of the hill below Q Troop's position lay a village which, from much later information, must have been Dragonea. A patrol was therefore organized to collect our empty water-bottles and go down to the village to get them refilled. Those of us who were not chosen for this trip occupied themselves in improving foxholes and re-cleaning and checking weapons, growing more and more thirsty all the while.

It was about one o'clock in the afternoon and the water party still hadn't returned when we heard the first sighing approach of incoming mortar bombs. We dived for our holes. Then came the urgent 'swish! swish! swish! swishes!' as they plummeted down into our area. The blast of the explosions hurled stones and hot metal fragments over our heads. We looked up to see clouds of whitish smoke drifting away from the points of impact, a short distance up the hill. Before the smoke had cleared, another salvo came over, then another, and another.

During initial training it had often been said that a soldier's best friend was his rifle – 'Take care of your rifle, son,' our veteran colour sergeant would say, 'and it will take care of you.' With this first experience of being under close mortar fire, we had no hesitation in giving pride of place to the humble entrenching tool. We ducked our heads down into our small holes as we heard more and more bombs arriving, then quickly bobbed them up again as soon as they had exploded, just in case there were any Germans coming in after them.

We weren't allowed to stay in the comparative safety of those holes for very long. The sound of small-arms fire had been added to the blasting explosions of bombs, and we were told that German infantry had been detected moving up the other side of the hill. Q Troop was switched over the ridge to be ready for them. We were given firing-positions overlooking the valley of La Molina. The view was expansive and impressive but we were more concerned about having had to leave the comparative safety of our holes and losing the shade of the trees. The

An aerial view of Punta Castellazzo and
'Commando Cove' (to the left of the
point) where Royal Marine Commandos
landed in the early hours of 9 July 1943

Skeleton beach defences 'folded like a concertina' when the
Canadians attacked Sicily. Landing craft on the right are
unloading tanks and supplies

A common sight in Sicily were the hundreds of 'Duces'
painted on the walls of houses

British troops passing bombed buildings as they march away
from the dock at Syracuse

One of the first Italian landing pictures taken showing the
arrival of the Sherman tanks

The viaduct at Vietri (the 'how's-about-it-
now' bridge crossed by 41 Commando in
the initial landing) after nine days of
German shellfire. On the bridge can be
seen an anti-tank gun and a truck from
46th Infantry Division

A jeep ambulance in the Salerno area transporting a wounded German

Men of 46th Infantry Division marching through Salerno towards Vietri to relieve the Commandos at La Molina

new positions were on the forward slope of the hilltop, out in the open, under the full glare of the sun – and we were still without water. There was no infantry activity to our immediate front: the Germans appeared to be concentrating their attention further to our left, towards the nose of the hill.

The usual infantry tactics for attacking a position are, first, to keep your enemy's heads down with anything you can throw at him – shells, bombs or bullets, while your assault troops move in as close as possible without being caught in the fire from their own people. Then, hopefully at the precise moment the covering fire is lifted, the infantrymen charge forward to catch the bemused enemy before he knows what is happening. At least that's how it should go, according to the book; it isn't always quite so simple in practice. Nevertheless, this basic technique invariably meant an alternation between mortar fire and small-arms fire in the forward positions.

As our hillside, to the Molina front and around towards the nose, was terraced in about six- or seven-feet drops, it would make any final assault by the Germans much more difficult, so we had some advantage there. And even after little more than an hour under fire, we were already becoming practised at distinguishing between the rather leisurely, 'swiiiiish, swiiiiish, swiiiiishes' of bombs that were going to land at a reasonably safe distance away and the fearsome, 'SSHH-SSHH-SSHH-SSHHs' of those whose trajectory was almost vertical and were going to end up dangerously close, so we knew just when to get really scared. In our exposed situation on the open hillside we had the additional, although not very helpful, information of knowing just when another batch of bombs was starting its flight towards us, as we could clearly hear the dull thumps as they were ejected from the mortar barrels.

While the activity remained around the inland end of the hill, those in our little sector had nothing much to do other than keep a sharp look-out and appraise the countryside spread out before us. Immediately to our front, the view of our hillside didn't extend beyond the second terrace down. After that, the many hundreds of feet to the valley bottom were hidden by the canopies of countless trees. To our right front, across the defile, maybe a mile away, was the steep barren face of another hill, towering up to a summit much higher than the one we were on. This too, we were assured, was in British hands, although we could see no signs of movement of any kind. To our left front there was an eagle's-eye view of a more open, flatter part of the valley, where we could see the road and railway track heading towards Cava. This view of the valley floor was cut off at a distance of perhaps 1½ miles from us, where the road curved round to the left to lose itself behind a long, low, grey-coloured building. The town of Vietri sul Mare, somewhere away to our right, was also hidden from view by wooded hills, and from time to time we saw puffs of white smoke billowing up above the trees in that direction which told us that there too German bombs or shells were falling.

For the Salerno operation, the Commando's Heavy Weapons Section was concentrating on its heavy machine-guns. Their rather short-ranged three-inch mortars had been left behind in Sicily, and we were being provided with mortar support by the Americans. Theirs were 4.2 inch weapons, similar in size to the Italian ones used against us on the first day in Sicily and with a similarly long range. From our vantage-point, overlooking La Molina, we were now to observe a reassuring demonstration of the Yanks' proficiency. At the point where the road to Cava disappeared from view behind the grey building, a German tank or self-propelled gun (SP) would, from time to time, emerge and commence firing down the valley in our general direction. It never had time to loose off more than one or two rounds before American mortar bombs were exploding in front of its nose, and back it would scurry to safety. As well as providing us with reassuring proof of the accuracy of the American mortar squad, that little cat-and-mouse game also provided a useful audio-comparison between the dull thumps of the German mortars and the sharp cracks of their high-velocity guns. We were learning.

But the blazing sun was burning our backs through the thin khaki drill uniforms. Trickles of sweat coursed from beneath steel helmets down faces and necks. Still without water, lips and throats were becoming increasingly parched. As the afternoon wore on, I searched my pockets again and again for the packet of Lifesavers which had certainly been there that morning. I was desperately reluctant to accept the fact that they had been lost in the general scuffling around, but never found them.

Then we had another diversion down on the valley floor. At about half-left from our position, a German mortar team moved into an open field and began to set up their weapons. This was an opportunity too good to miss: we opened fire with our rifles, and from a short distance to our left a bren also started to chatter away. All to no effect. Hardly had we realized that the range must have been too great for us than one of the Vickers heavy machine-guns began firing from a position still further along the hill to our left. We saw no obvious casualties but the Germans certainly got the message and disappeared in great haste behind an adjacent hedge.

We were lying well spaced out as usual, and this brought our little corner of the war down to a very personal level. Of the whole Commando I could see only two men – Scouse Haggerty and Killer Barker. Killer was about five yards away to my left, and Hag about five yards further on. Jack Horsfield and Bill Marshall were similarly placed to my right, but slightly to the rear and not visible unless I turned my head through about 120 degrees. Somewhere within calling distance lay Corporal Ted Malt, our immediate link with the chain of command that would pass us our orders. But we received surprisingly few of those and hardly any items of information after being told, 'Right! – Down, here! Fire when a target presents itself.' Of the remaining men in the unit, where they were positioned, what they were doing, how many were already casualties, we knew nothing.

As to just how close the Germans were, we could only guess, but they were clearly not far off, judging from the medley of exploding hand-grenades and the small-arms fire from a number of different automatic weapons, British and German, which alternated with the periods of mortaring. The activity was still being concentrated around the nose of the hill. Absorbing the entire range of background noises and witnessing the happenings down in the valley below us occupied only one part of our consciousness. Throughout it all our prime concern remained the continual search and re-search of the edge of that second terrace down the hill for the first sight of a German coal-scuttle helmet.

After a particularly extended plastering of mortar bombs, we heard a renewed crackling of rifle fire and sustained bren-gun fire break out around the nose of the hill. This was joined, almost immediately, by the much deeper, 'tunktunktunktunktunk' of the Vickers machine-guns. Obviously another infantry attack was developing. Suddenly we were called to our feet again – to get back to the other side of the hill as the Germans were also coming up there. We raced back over the ridge and were directed towards the left front of the nose, where we were pleased to be able to flop into somebody else's foxholes; it was also a relief to get back into the shade amongst the trees. There was no doubt that the enemy infantry were very close. We could hear their guttural shouts, and the fantastically rapid 'brrrrrrrrrrrrrrrpps' of fire from their Schmeisser machine-pistols (or 'electric guns', as we called them) were disconcertingly close.

Our attackers were completely hidden from view by the vines, the trees and the terraces. We fired at the sound of their voices, at any slight movement in the foliage and, probably, at many innocent shadows. The Germans may well have been having the same problems but dealing with them with rather less success, as we weren't doing any shouting. Certainly most of the bullets coming our way seemed to do little more than slash the leaves from the trees above us and scatter them onto our heads. The general din of the medley of crackling rifle fire, plus the incessant splattering of the Commando's and the Germans' automatic weapons, was again interspersed with the blasting explosions of hand-grenades. Our combined efforts must have been effective. The small-arms fire gradually petered out as the Germans pulled back their infantry once again, to allow the mortars to take over and resume the softening-up treatment.

From the intensity of the ensuing deluge of explosives it seemed likely that the number of mortars being brought to bear upon us had been increased or, more probably, that some SPs were now joining in. Under such concentrated fire it was impossible for their infantry to put in an attack, so we kept our heads well down below ground-level, then popped them up at any slight lull in case we were being rushed. Split up as the Commando was, and scattered over the varying levels of the hilltop, there were, once more, very few of our own chaps to be seen. Each man's world shrank down to the size of the slit trench in which he crouched. Since moving over the hilltop for the second time, my particular little sector seemed to be out of immediate contact with the rest of the Troop. Captain Stott, we had been told, had gone off with a few men on a reconnaissance patrol early in the morning but we had received no news of their return. Nor had we heard anything from Lieutenant Haydon since the start of the mortaring early in the afternoon.

Somewhere to my right as I crouched in my new hole, I could from time to time hear the voice of Lieutenant Lloyd, in charge of No. 8 section, shouting commands and words of encouragement to his men. Then, in a lull after yet another prolonged barrage of mortar bombs, I heard Lloydie's voice for the last time in a much higher, almost hysterical key. 'Come on, Q Troop,' he was bawling. 'Let's get those bloody mortars!' Even a humble marine like myself realized that this made no sense at all. The mortars could have been anything up to two miles or more away and in almost any direction to our front that you cared to choose. It would have been virtually impossible to find them, even without the presence of an unknown number of German infantrymen, waiting just beyond the bursting bombs, for the opportunity of assaulting our position.

I wasn't a member of Lieutenant Lloyd's section, but the fact that he had called upon 'Q Troop' rather than his own section gave me a niggling uneasiness about whether I was expected to join in. By the normal chain of command I would have received my orders from Lieutenant Haydon, my section commander, or from Captain Stott, the Troop commander himself. I looked around to confer with someone but couldn't see a soul. There had, I knew, been a gradual diminution in the number of men near me – wounded going back for attention, others called away to take messages, NCOs going off to try to find out what was happening – but now I appeared to be completely on my own. At first I decided that I should await more positive orders to move but, as the minutes passed and no one came to instruct or collect me, I began to feel completely isolated.

Without any idea of what was happening but realizing that the situation on the hill had become rather crucial, I guessed that the place for the Commando to re-form in order to deal with it would be somewhere up on the higher ground. Taking advantage of an easing of the bombardment, I started to move up to make contact. After only a dozen yards or so, I came upon one of the Commando, huddled against a rock in a small hollow in the hillside, trying, one-handedly, to fix a field dressing on a messy gash in his left shoulder. I completed the job for him and watched, with a slight twinge of envy, as he started his painful way back down the hill in search of the Regimental Aid Post, before continuing my way upwards.

The easing-off of the mortaring had pressaged another infantry attack. As the splattering of small-arms fire started up again, I came across a group of six or seven marines in firing-positions around the edge of a shallow depression in the ground. It was a great relief to have linked up with somebody, and I thankfully slithered in beside them.

The crackle of rifle fire and the chatter of various automatic weapons rose in intensity, and smoke from bursting grenades once more began to drift over the hilltop. Almost immediately we were precipitately joined by one of the Vickers machine-gunners, who rolled into our position after having had to abandon his gun when the rest of the crew had been killed. In his hand he clutched the 'lock' of the weapon – standard procedure if a machine-gun had to be left behind, to prevent its being used by the enemy.

At about the same moment, Corporal Pryor came on the scene with two other men of Q Troop. He understood that most of the unit had already been pulled back some distance from the nose. There were, apparently, very few men left in that area, so he widened our defensive position by moving us into a double extended line, to await developments. From him we learned that Lieutenant Lloyd had in fact gone ahead with his foolhardy attack but had got no further than the first terrace before he, and the two men with him, had been cut down in a hail of bullets. The section sergeant, Sergeant Cole, had then taken over command and stopped any of the others from following.

We were now lying prone on the open hillside, with the usual five yards or so between men, when a cloud of white smoke billowed up from a clump of bushes some thirty yards from us, slightly downhill to our left front. A bren which had been firing from that position suddenly stopped. We tensed and a 'Here they come!' flashed through my brain as shadowy figures emerged from the smoke. I squinted over the sights and had taken first pressure on the trigger when a sudden yell stopped us, 'Hold your fire! They're our chaps!' Just in time – it was the bren group pulling back. They took up a position on the right of our line, further up the hill. Now we could be certain that anything that moved to our front would be 'theirs'. We licked our parched lips and waited.

It was evening by this time and, as the minutes ticked slowly by, we began to realize that the hill was quietening down. There had been a noticeable easing-off of small-arms fire, and the bursts of grenades had become much less frequent. We could scarcely believe that there would not be another attack but, as the shadows lengthened, firing gradually subsided altogether and, for the first time since early afternoon, it was all quiet on the hilltop.

In the deepening dusk it became possible to move about again. Officers and NCOs gathered the remnants of the

Commando together, and we were withdrawn a few dozen yards further from the nose to concentrate around the highest point of the hill. Here, in groups of three men – to alternate the watches during the night – we were arranged into a rough circle, of perhaps seventy or eighty yards diameter. I was again positioned on the La Molina side, although in the darkness I could see very little of it. We were still without water, so it wasn't easy to get the meagre remnants of our forty-eight-hour ration – little more than a few biscuits – down to our hungry bellies. Nevertheless, it was a great relief to be able to stretch out full length in the peaceful obscurity of the darkness, and breathe deeply of the cool night air.

Suddenly our muscles tensed again. The silence had been broken by a guarded shout, coming from somewhere further around our perimeter. It was undoubtedly German, calling out what sounded like 'Ecksy Companee?' This was followed by a single rifle shot, then all was quiet again. We looked at one another queryingly until word came around that a German officer, presumably under the impression that the hill was in their hands, had walked into our position. He had been killed by Jock More.

Other pieces of information filtered through to us in the darkness. Colonel Lumsden had been badly wounded in the thigh, and some others had also been injured when a direct hit had demolished the headquarters bunker in Vietri, early in the action. As for our Troop commander, Captain Stott, at that time we knew only that he was still missing. It was later confirmed that he too was dead. We were told that his body had been found in an outhouse down in the village, below the position Q Troop had first occupied on the hill. It was said that his patrol had bumped into a party of Germans and that there had been a running fight around the houses. Our chaps were split up, and it was assumed that, after being wounded, Captain Stott had crawled or been dragged under cover, where he died.

Lieutenant Haydon, my section officer, had been badly wounded in the very first salvo of mortar bombs, although he had stayed on the hill, in a shallow depression in the rock face, for most of the day. With Lieutenant Lloyd also killed, Q Troop was left without any commissioned officers. Alec Kennedy, one of the Troop bren-gunners and also our (unofficial) piper, was amongst those killed. Alec had been a particular friend of mine. When stationed at Troon I had visited his family in Glasgow, where he had worked as a packer for one of the city newspapers. James Smith of No. 8 section was also dead – he had been a very good swimmer who participated in many of our 'O Group' frolics in the Mediterranean at Aci Castello. Throughout the Commando there were many dead, wounded and missing; the officers, it seemed, had fared particularly badly, and there were few of them left.

Later that night Vietri sul Mare received more attention from the German artillery – it wasn't until after the war that I appreciated that their primary target had been the viaduct we crossed on the first day, which had been an important Allied supply route. Lying in the still darkness on our hill, we could hear the surprisingly leisurely swishing of projectiles in flight down the valley in front of us. Some appeared to carry an auxiliary charge, to increase their range, as they seemed to emit additional 'swiisshes' as they passed us. There was no way of telling whether they were mortar bombs or artillery shells – they all gave the same muffled thumps when they exploded. As on the previous nights, there was the continuous grumbling roll of gunfire from the main landing-area. Things were not going at all well down there, but we still had no idea of the actual situation and had received no indication of when they might get through to us at La Molina.

The night passed quietly enough. We took it in turns to spend an hour on look-out while the other two slept – passing a luminous wristwatch over to the next one to stay awake. Once again dawn stand-to dragged by very slowly and passed without an attack. As soon as it was full daylight, patrols were pushed forward to the outer edges of the hill. Nothing was encountered, so we were spread out to re-occupy the whole position once more.

Water was again our first urgent concern, but much more so this time as we hadn't had a drink for about twenty-four hours. Then, miraculously and without any explanation, the water-bottles re-appeared, filled to the brim – although they didn't stay that way for very long. Now food became top priority. We hunted through the pockets of our bush jackets and searched ammunition pouches, fishing out the last few remaining biscuits to share for breakfast.

By daylight it could be seen that the German who had stumbled into our position was from the vaunted Hermann Goering Division, so we knew whom we were up against. It was also realized that what he had been calling out was 'Sechzig Kompanie' – 'Sixtieth Company'. The morning advanced slowly, quietly and hungrily. We waited expectantly for a renewal of the attacks – and for the arrival of some food, but, as hour followed hour without incident, our expectancy changed to puzzlement. Then somebody realized that it was Saturday, and we laughingly concluded that the Hermann Goering Division had gone off to Naples on weekend leave. Others had a better idea: the Fifth Army had sorted out their problems down in the beachhead and were now pushing forward to link up with us, so the German forces in our area had been pulled back.

Early in the afternoon there seemed to be little doubt that the second alternative had been correct. A long string of men of the Lincolnshire Regiment and the King's Own Yorkshire Light Infantry trudged into our position, sweating profusely after their gruelling climb up from Vietri. We gave them a warm, heartfelt welcome – even before they gave us some of their food. It was never revealed to us just where they had come from, whether up the coast from the main beaches or perhaps from another landing at Vietri, but we weren't particularly interested. At the time we had much more important things to occupy our minds, like being pulled back to the seaward end of the hill to be put into reserve, then receiving a thin slice of corned beef and two compo biscuits per man – the relief column was clearly on British, not American, rations. Even as we were eating the food, the Army chaps (it later transpired that they were part of the 138th Infantry

Brigade of the 46th 'Cherry Pickers' Division) started work with their full-sized picks and shovels to replace our small foxholes with the much larger trenches they preferred. We sat with our legs dangling in some ready-made holes on a lightly tree-clad rearward slope of the hill, overlooking the Mediterranean. It was Saturday afternoon and we had nothing to do and nowhere to go. Then a little entertainment, from our point of view at least, was laid on. The monitor HMS *Roberts*, lying close inshore – but perhaps about two miles horizontally and some 3,000 feet vertically from where we sat – started a 'shoot'. Designed specifically for engaging targets on shore and in particular for bombarding coastal defences, those shallow-draught ships (only about eleven feet compared with the twenty-seven or twenty-eight feet of a battleship) were little more than floating platforms for their twin fifteen-inch guns. Firing shells which weighed a ton each and with a range of some twenty-three miles, they could drop their visiting cards a long way from the sea. As those guns fired, the concussion from each salvo, even at the distance we were away from them, was sufficient to shake the ground around the top of our hole and send little rivulets of dry earth trickling down the sides. Short moments later we heard the snarling, spinning shells pass high above our heads like angry omnibuses, and after a further short interval came the heavy, dull thumps as they exploded, goodness knows how many miles inland. We had no idea what the target was that day but couldn't help feeling a twinge of pity for anyone on the receiving end.

Those same guns had actually accomplished the major part of the task the Commando had been given to do behind the German lines to the north of Catania in Sicily. They had carried out a shoot in the vicinity of Taormina, where their shells had caused a landslide which effectively blocked both the coastal road and the railway. This would appear to be a much better way of doing that sort of job than putting a few hundred marines ashore to stop the traffic.

After the *Roberts* episode, the day continued hot and peaceful. As the afternoon tailed off into evening, we continued to wait expectantly for the arrival of our rations, before settling down for the night. By the time daylight had faded completely, without any food, we had passed the stage of expectation – but still carried on hoping. Dusk had given way to total darkness when we were abruptly roused by the completely unexpected order 'All right! On your feet! Get rigged! We're moving off.' In a matter of minutes, puzzled and none too pleased, we were stumbling in single file down the black hillside. Not knowing, not even seeing, where we were going, the march seemed interminable but we allowed ourselves to be comforted by the thought that surely there would be something to eat at the end of it. Around midnight we eventually turned off the road and were told that this was where we would spend the night.

As a bivouac area it was unlike anything we could possibly have imagined. There was a concrete floor and, in the semi-darkness, it resembled nothing so much as the aisle of a lofty cathedral. Then we realized that we had been deposited beneath the tall arches of a viaduct, and there was just sufficient light for us to see that one entire side of the colossal structure (obviously the one facing the sea) had been draped with camouflage netting, giving the whole thing the appearance of the backdrop for some mammoth stage production.

As we were fallen out, each man received a packet of K rations. After hurriedly dropping off our gear, we squatted on the ground and stuffed ourselves with spam, sweetcorn, cheese, biscuits and candy, without any thought for the morrow. In spite of having no more than a concrete pavement for a bed, we stretched out blissfully for sleep. Before dropping off we became dimly aware of 'noises off' – explosions and small-arms fire, which could very well have come from 'our' hill – but that was no longer any concern of ours. We fell asleep happy in the thought that our part in the Salerno landing was over. The Commando Brigade's responsibility for La Molina had been handed over to the Army. It was two days later than had been expected, but we were on our way back to the beach.

The few facts regarding the death of Captain Stott, so far as I was aware of them at the time, are set out above. Eric Morris, in his book *Salerno – A Military Fiasco* (Hutchinson, 1983) writes: '...The Germans poured through the gap, broke into the village of Dragonea and A Troop was surrounded. The reserve troop (Q Troop) which was positioned to launch its own counter-attack, stormed down the hill and into the village. Martin Stott was killed at the head of his men and Wilkinson saw a section leader lieutenant hurl a grenade at a group of advancing Germans. One of the latter fired his machine pistol and cut down the young officer even as he and the others were killed by the grenade.'

When this counter-attack took place, and how it was that neither I nor any of the others close to me during that day was not called upon to join in, is a mystery to me.

'Stottie' was over medium height, lean, wiry and with such reserves of stamina that on a long route march we sometimes wondered if he had a secret supply of benzedrine pep pills to keep him going. He was always raring to go, so it was ironic that he, of all people, should miss the Sicily landing because of a simple engine failure. But it wasn't altogether surprising that he had been killed on his first day in action – if he had behaved then with the same rash impetuosity he invariably displayed during our training exercises.

Early in the previous year, as a lieutenant in charge of the carrier platoon (an amalgam of bren-gun carriers and motor-cyclists) of the 8th Battalion Royal Marines, prior to the formation of 41 Commando, he had personally led the motor-cycle section (of which I was the anti-tank rifleman) during a brigade attack on Dartmouth. A dashing sortie into the town, braving fusillades of blank cartridges fired at us through the hedges by the local Home Guard unit, had culminated in abandoning our bikes to make a frontal assault, through an entanglement of 'Dannert' concertina barbed wire, up a hillock being defended by cadets of the Naval Academy. By chance, the brigadier had chosen that hill as his vantage-point from which to watch the course of the battle. As we reached the summit, I was close enough to hear him greet our platoon officer. 'Marvellous show, Stott,' he boomed. 'You'd have won the VC for that – but you wouldn't have been around to see it!'

Captain Stott has no known grave and is commemorated by name on Panel 102 of the Plymouth Naval Memorial; he was aged twenty-two.

Lieutenant Haydon, who was only nineteen at the time, was awarded the DSO for his bravery on that day. A press cutting from the *Daily Mirror* of 9 February 1944 includes the following sentences: 'During a heavy counter-attack, in which the enemy strafed the position with mortar fire, Lieutenant Haydon received a serious shrapnel wound. ... He calmly directed the defence of the position and inspired his men to counter the attack, in which he was wounded again by a bullet in the thigh.'

Peter Haydon returned to the Commando but was killed in the Walcheren operation to open the Port of Antwerp in November 1944; he is buried in the Bergen op Zoom War Cemetery in the Netherlands.

Lieutenant Lloyd is buried in the Salerno War Cemetery; he was twenty-one.

'Lloydie' had been Q Troop's expert on infantry tactics. He was the officer to be sent on the appropriate training course when any changes in the standard infantry manoeuvres were being promulgated by the Army Council. After the course, he would pass on his recently acquired knowledge in a series of sub-section demonstrations. At that stage of the war, infantry tactics were based on the bren-group/rifle-group drill, which assumed that the officer in charge knew precisely where the enemy position was, so he would decide whether the riflemen should attack from the left (left flanking) or from the right (right flanking). He would also choose precisely where the bren-group should be positioned to provide covering fire. The whole procedure would be initiated in a single sentence, such as, 'Enemy position edge of wood, left at nine o'clock – right flanking bren-group – there!', and off we would all go at the double. Lloydie loved it – he would even cheer on the Troop football team by thwacking his leg with his cane, bawling, 'Attack! Attack! Attack!'

Alec Kennedy has no known grave and is commemorated by name on Panel 93 of the Portsmouth Naval Memorial; he was twenty-one.

10   *Back up the Hill*

When we awoke next morning, our resting-place was bright with dappled sunshine and by daylight looked even more like a stage setting than when we arrived during the night. And now the *dramatis personae* could be seen – scores of dirty and dishevelled marines. With their untidy heaps of weapons and equipment, they stood out in sharp contrast to the clean, stark whiteness of the pavement and the tapering concrete piers of the viaduct that curved into rounded arches high above our heads. There was water a-plenty, so we luxuriated in a wash and shave – with the titillating aroma of American coffee wafting around the bivouac area. Then a leisurely breakfast on the few remnants of the previous night's pack of K rations, washed down with our first hot drink since landing. Was that less than four days ago? It seemed like weeks.

As the sun climbed high into a cloudless sky, the titanic efforts of the camouflage experts became fully appreciated. Not only had they achieved an impressive engineering feat but the huge expanse of netting and coloured canvas strips provided a welcome protection from the hot Italian sun. We idly watched the few curious civilians passing our camp and wondered how we would be allowed to spend the day – probably a make-and-mend to wash our socks and underclothes, we thought. And, with the sparkling Mediterranean only a few hundred feet below us, there was surely the likelihood of a Sunday by the seaside with a long, cool swim. Even as an ill-defined thought it seemed too good to be true. It was. The blow, when it came, was almost physical as the rasping bellow of authority jolted us back to reality. 'All right, lads. Don't start any dhobying. Clean your weapons and pack your kit. Be ready to move off in half an hour!' Mouths dropped open in dismay. 'Where now, corp?' we wanted to know, but the only response from Jan Maley was, 'You'll find out soon enough.'

Our departure was simply the arrival in reverse – a packet of K rations per man and *exeunt* left'. Then we were marching back in the direction from which we had arrived only a few hours earlier. That was sufficient to confirm the already strong suspicion that we were going back up that same bloody hill. Detailed explanations of the whys and wherefores of things were rarely forthcoming, and this was no exception. The only information to be gleaned was that the hill had almost been recaptured by the Germans during the previous night. It was now being held by No. 2 Commando, and we were on our way to join them. We didn't get to know what had happened in our absence and never again saw the Army chaps who had taken over from us. It wasn't until after the war that I learned that they had been called back to their brigade to help stem a German counter-attack in their own sector, to the north-east of Salerno. What was abundantly clear to us, on that Sunday morning, was that very few of the Army had in fact arrived in Vietri sul Mare and that 41 Commando was back in business.

Arriving at the foot of the hill we found, once again, that there was a dump of machine-gun ammunition to be carried up. For a change, however, we were to ascend by way of the vine terraces – here again, no reason was given. Some changes may be as good as a rest, but this wasn't one of them. Each move, from one terrace to the next, meant first passing up your rifle and box of ammunition, then a 'lift and tug' procedure to move the lines of sweating men up the hillside. Putting a foot in the clasped hands of the man behind and grasping the hand of the one already up there, a co-ordinated lift from below and heave from above would land you on the next terrace. As soon as you arrived, it was your turn to haul up the man below, then make a step for the man in front. We found that seven or eight feet vertically, followed by about fifteen horizontally, time and again and again, was a much more exhausting procedure than the long, steady trudge of the previous route. It was probably a shorter and perhaps a quicker way of getting to the top, but it was a hard slog before we found ourselves back in familiar territory. One unmistakable landmark was the body of the German who had stumbled into our position on Friday night. Apparently no one had had time to bury him; he still lay where he had fallen, fully dressed in multi-coloured camouflaged jacket, trousers and peaked cap.

It was hot, sunny and peaceful on the hilltop, and everything looked very much the same as it had on the previous afternoon. The only noticeable difference was the number of commodious infantry trenches that had appeared in the groundscape. Infantry holes were excavated to much more generous proportions than ours – they were usually for two or more men and could be of the order of six feet long by two wide and as much as five feet deep. Each dimension was a reason for our not liking them. The larger plan area presented a bigger target, and the increased depth made them so much more difficult to vacate in a hurry should the need arise. With our puny entrenching tools we excavated foxholes to minimum dimensions. They were tailor-made to the width of the shoulders, not much more than three feet long and hardly two feet deep. By kneeling down and bending forward, even in such small confines, there was room enough to keep the whole of your body below ground-level. The fact that such a posture was simultaneously suitable for both protection and praying was not overlooked and often appreciated.

We learned that No. 2 Commando was already positioned around the nose of the hill, although we couldn't see anything of them because of the contours and vegetation. On our arrival, No. 41 appeared to be strung out over the ridge and part way down both sides, some eighty or ninety yards behind them, to give depth to the Brigade position.

Once again I was on the backward slope away from La Molina. There were no more than four other marines to be seen in the immediate vicinity, and together we formed the extreme left flank of the Commando defence line. Three of my companions were Londoners – Bill Marshall from Wembley and Harry Weiss from Bow, plus Killer Barker who came from Romford. The fourth man was Jock More, the Scotsman who had disposed of *'Sechzig Kompanie'*.

Our five individual holes were arranged in an irregular group, because of the rough terrain. They lay between five and ten yards from each other and were at varying distances down the hillside from a narrow track (mine was only a foot away) which meandered up to the forward areas. On the uphill side of the track, immediately to our right, a vertical outcrop of rock, rising to a height of some twelve to fifteen feet, effectively cut us off from the rest of the Commando line, which continued up and over the hill. Some twenty yards beyond this outcrop, the rock face gave way to the steep, grassy slope of the hillside, and about thirty yards or so further forward this bulged out into a rounded, tree-clad knoll extending across our front. The track curved around this knoll, upwards and to the left, before being lost from sight in a jumble of bushes and trees. To our left, the lightly wooded hillside fell away steeply, the ground disappearing from view at distances varying from only about forty yards to some sixty yards, and beyond that we could see no more than the tops of the trees growing lower down the steep slope.

The remainder of Sunday passed quietly enough as we lay watching and waiting – but, more particularly, listening. The Germans were obviously only a few hundred yards away, somewhere down the hill to our left in the direction of Dragonea, completely out of sight but well within earshot. We heard the comings and goings of their wheeled transport and, much more ominous, the clankings of tracked vehicles – possibly tanks but more probably 88mm self-propelled guns. German voices, too, carried up to us quite clearly. None of us could understand what was being said except when some shouted words of command, which we could recognize as such simply by their tone, ended up with, *'Heil Hitler!'* Then we amused ourselves by blowing strings of 'raspberries' in that general direction. Darkness gradually swallowed up the hill, and throughout the night everything remained quiet and undisturbed as we took it in turns at keeping a sharp look-out, ears strained for the slightest sound, and sleeping on the ground close by our holes. The Brigade was stood to in the pre-dawn darkness, every man alert in his hole, weapon at the ready. With each minute seeming like ten, we waited silent and motionless as the sun, with exasperating slowness, gradually lightened the night sky. This time there was to be no stand-down for breakfast. Before daylight had fully established itself, the stillness was abruptly shattered by German guns and mortars opening up a devastating fire. Everyone crouched low in their holes as shells and bombs began plastering the hilltop. The sharp swishes of falling missiles and their shattering explosions soon built up into one unimaginable din. The ground quivered under the pounding, and the air was torn by a rising crescendo of noise and jagged splinters of steel.

We five, on the extreme left of the Commando line, had the special responsibilty of watching out for any out-flanking movement of the enemy. This meant that we had to keep our heads above ground until the last possible moment as the bombs and shells were screeching in (lest the enemy was using those last few seconds to work his way closer), then get them back up above ground again immediately after the explosions, just in case that had been the last salvo before the infantry assault. From the blasts of the slightly more distant missiles came the angry whines which heralded the approach of slashing bomb splinters soon to be lacerating the foliage about us. Ears, by this time, were fully attuned to the different 'swishes' of those bombs which were going to explode harmlessly, so far as you were concerned, a score or more yards away and the imminent arrival of the very close ones which meant 'Head down in a big hurry!'

The brief intervals of time – between the first intimation that an incoming batch of bombs was going to land much too close for comfort, and the moment after they had exploded, when you thankfully realized that you were still all in one piece – became more and more nerve-racking. It was always difficult to decide just when it might be safe to pop your head up for another look around, and the instinctive temptation not to do so at all became stronger and stronger. Exposed on the surface of the ground we could hardly have survived for more than a few minutes, but squashed low in our foxholes there was reasonable protection from anything short of a direct hit.

With no officers of our own Troop remaining, we had been placed under the command of Captain Wilkinson of A Troop. Our only tenuous link with the rest of the Commando was through his disembodied voice, coming to us from a hole somewhere to the rear and further up the hill. Near him he had a signaller with the Troop radio, a bulky, back-packed '18 set' – these were temperamental beasts at the best of times and half-useless amongst hills and trees, but some information seemed to be getting through. From time to time Captain Wilkinson would call out, asking if we were still OK and, equally important from our point of view, letting us know that we had not been left completely on our own. After perhaps half an hour, when the barrage became even more concentrated in our area, we heard the opening crackle and splatter of small-arms fire coming from the nose of the hill. No. 2 Commando was under attack – and the German gunners and mortar men appeared to have increased the range to concentrate their explosives further back along the ridge. We lost track of time. There was nothing to do but crouch low and keep as good a look-out to the front and left flank as falling bombs would permit.

It was still quite early in the morning, although there was warmth in the sun which had eased its way above the trees, when we heard Captain Wilkinson bawling to us that No. 2 was being pulled back through our position and warning us not to shoot at them. Almost immediately ten or twelve men came racing down the track, intense strain showing on their sweat-stained faces. Despite the warmth of the sun they were still wearing, on top of their khaki drill, the blue woollen jerseys they had put on against the chill of the night and which they clearly hadn't had an opportunity to remove. Some flopped down near us for a short while but one trio hurtled past without any pause. Two were running, each grasping an ankle of a wounded comrade. Lying on his back, he was being dragged over the rough, stony ground like a sack of potatoes. As they disappeared to the rear, another blue-jerseyed commando flopped down on the track beside my hole to let me know that he was the last man of No. 2 on this sector of the hill – anything behind him was German. He lay beside me for a few minutes, both of us firing at any suspected movement in the bushes further up the track, then he too moved back to join the survivors of his section.

Bullets were now zipping wildly about us, slicing leaves from the nearby branches. We were shooting at anything suspicious, although vision was restricted by the bushes and trees and blurred with the smoke from explosions. There was nothing that could be positively identified as a German, but if anything moved, I fired. On one occasion I opened rapid fire at something coming out of the undergrowth above the knoll, about thirty yards to my front, and must have loosed off at least three rounds before recognizing it as nothing more than a British fighting-order pack, dislodged by an exploding bomb or grenade and rolling madly down the hillside.

The Germans had become vociferous again, calling to one another and shouting words of command, but this time they were immeasurably closer than on the previous day. We never did find out whether this shouting business was an attempt to lower our morale or to raise their own or if it just happened to be part of the Teutonic make-up. Whatever the reason for it, the shouting made it abundantly clear that Jerry was only a few dozen yards away and, as we couldn't see him, it was helpful to be able to fire in the general direction of the voices. Once again the long and fantastically rapid bursts of fire from their Schmeissers, sounding as though the bullets were tied together with very short lengths of string, were awesomely close. In comparison, the deliberate splutterings of our own bren-guns, firing away almost continuously, somewhere further up the hill, sounded pathetically slow.

Fortunately, the Germans must have been having the same visibility problems as we were. Once I saw the spurts of earth kicked up by a stream of bullets running down the track in my general direction. As I ducked automatically, they were striking the ground only inches away from the edge of my hole, spattering soil particles onto the top of my steel helmet. It could have been nothing more than a random burst: it is pretty certain that aimed shots would not have missed.

Captain Wilkinson continued to keep in touch. 'Are you all right, chaps?' he would shout. 'Things are going OK – just stay put.' We didn't think that things were going particularly well – but we weren't being paid to think. A little later he called out, 'Are there any of No. 2 still down there with you?' I looked around and, seeing a chap in a blue jersey lying on his stomach a little further downhill to my left front, called out, 'Just one, sir!' But another voice quickly chipped in, saying, 'I'm afraid he must be dead, sir. He hasn't moved for half an hour.' After that we were told to fire at any blue jerseys seen moving to our front. A group of Germans, wearing jerseys taken from the dead of No. 2 Commando, had almost achieved a breakthrough higher up the hill.

The combined firing of the Commando had clearly deterred the Germans from coming in any closer. The small-arms fire eased off and the bombs started coming in again – their infantry had been pulled back to let the mortars have another go. By this time our leg muscles were cramped and aching with the prolonged kneeling, but there was nothing we could safely do about it. At least we had plenty of exercise from the waist upwards.

During one of the short lulls Sergeant Cole paid us a flying visit. Flopping down alongside me, he asked, 'Want any fags?' When I nodded a grateful 'Yes, please!' he dropped two packets of 'Victory Vs' into my hole. 'Here you are then. Padre's been scrounging.' As he flitted away, I wondered vaguely about paying for them but was more interested in starting a chain-smoking session which lasted for the next few hours. That particular brand of cigarette wasn't greatly sought-after, for they were made in India and had a distinctly non-Virginian taste, but we were in no position to be choosy. With a packet lying open on the edge of the hole, it was a simple matter to light a fresh one from the stub of the old, using only the left hand, while still keeping a sharp look-out. There was never any let-up in the continuous search for any movement on the bush-covered hill to our front and left flank – rifle in the right hand, always pointed forward, finger crooked around the trigger.

It would probably have been some time around noon, the swishing and bursting of bombs and shells having once again given way to alarmingly close small-arms fire, when we heard a rapid series of explosions that sent puffs of white smoke billowing up through the bushes and trees, only about sixty or seventy yards ahead of us. In a matter of seconds the individual puffs had thickened into a dense white curtain, stretching across the whole of our front. I quickly lit another cigarette and flexed the fingers of my right hand, before grasping the rifle again, convinced that German infantry would soon be charging through the smoke. Jock More, crouching in his hole a few yards in front of me, had the same idea and yelled out, 'Look out! The bastards'll be coming through that, any second.' But we were wrong. Captain Wilkinson's voice came through again, advising us that this wasn't the German smokescreen we had imagined but a barrage of phosphorous bombs being put down by the American mortar squad. We sighed with relief but quickly realized that someone was taking a pretty hefty risk – with our lives at stake – by calling for that kind of support so close to their own troops. Yet we mentally thanked them for it. This was the first intimation we had had of any supporting fire from our side on that hill, and once again we had to hand it to the Yanks – they didn't put a bomb wrong.

As the white wall of smoke continued to grow under the rain of American bombs, the undergrowth caught fire, and the crackle of burning bushes was added to the general hubbub. On top of everything else we now began to hear alternating screams and low moans of agony from a wounded German caught somewhere in the burning phosphorus who must have been unable to get away. The harrowing sounds went on for a sickeningly long time while we asked ourselves time and again why his mates couldn't do something for him. When the poor fellow's cries eventually stopped, our relief was probably not so much for the end of his sufferings as for the wholly selfish reason that we would no longer have to listen to him. After the war I learned that the Germans had accused the Americans of contravening the Geneva Convention as to chemical warfare by using those particular bombs.

Bullets continued to fly around at intervals, and the bursting of bombs, shells and hand-grenades never seemed to stop for very long. At no time was it quiet enough to risk leaving your hole for any of the calls of nature, so all natural functions had to be carried out where you were.

As the Germans were now getting some mortaring in reply, we felt that things were not quite so one-sided, but the automatic tensing of nerves and muscles at the approach of each batch of bombs was having its effect on us. It became increasingly tempting to put your head below ground-level at every 'swwwiiiissssshhh', whether or not it sounded as if it were going to land close by. It also became more and more difficult to push it up again after the latest batch of explosions. There was a growing temptation to close your eyes, sink deep into the earth and stay there until the whole infernal business had come to an end.

Things dragged on with no great change until, at perhaps two o'clock in the afternoon, the small-arms fire died away again and even the mortaring seemed to have eased off. There was a hail from Captain Wilkinson to tell us that a counter-attack was being organized, in collaboration with some Army troops. Infantry, from goodness knows where, were being positioned down in the valley to our left rear. The Commando was in radio communication with the attacking troops, and when they had advanced so as to be in line with us, we were to get up and move forward too. We didn't know whether or not to be pleased about this but had no say in the matter and realized that it should sort something out, one way or another. As the time for the attack drew near, the American mortars opened up again, giving the hill in front of us a concentrated plastering – of high explosives this time. Then we received the command 'Fix bayonets!' and, as the last Yankee bombs exploded, were ordered to get up and go.

It was a wrench to leave those holes, in which we had crouched for about eight solid hours, but up we jumped and raced forward. With amazed relief, we found that there were no bullets to greet us. After only a few strides we passed an abandoned Spandau machine-gun and were startled to see just how close the Germans had been. Then we came upon three or four of their dead, and some bodies of No. 2 Commando. We were still running on, but it was now clear that the Hermann Goering boys had withdrawn. Reaching the nose of the hill, we re-occupied the forward slit trenches. The whole position was back in our hands.

Almost instantaneously, the hilltop seemed to be flooded with British troops. Who they were and where they had come from, we had no idea, nor did we have any great interest. They were taking over, and we were only too happy to be stood down and be able to walk back to the rear of the hill, where we were put in reserve and given something to eat. We flopped into some Army holes to begin to unwind, and for once a mug of compo tea was drunk with relish. I was sharing an unusually large excavation with Bill Marshall and Killer Barker – it was about six feet square and two to three feet deep. After hours of being bent double in our cramped little holes, it was an immense relief to be able to stretch out full length. But the enemy mortars were still active, so it wasn't possible to relax completely. In the early evening the mortar fire was stepped up, and it appeared that our area was receiving special treatment. Then we wished we had been given a hole that wasn't quite so big.

After a full day of mortar bombs, most of us were jumpy, and the strain of these latest salvoes was proving too much for Bill. For quite some time we had noticed that he was quiet and withdrawn, lying slumped against the far side of the hole. But now his whole body began to shake and twitch involuntarily. His face was expressionless, and although his eyes were wide open, they were glassy, staring straight ahead and totally uncomprehending. From his lips came a noise which was part moan and part whimper. He reacted automatically to the falling bombs, his hunched shoulders contracting even more tightly at every swish. His shaking became more violent and uncontrolled the closer the bombs fell. This was our first experience of 'shellshock' or 'battle fatigue', when something snaps inside a man's head and his brain gives up the struggle to keep control. I cradled Bill in my arms, trying to calm his convulsions and bring him back to reality, but it was useless. It appeared as if his mind was a complete blank, unable to understand anything we said and leaving him without any power of speech of his own.

We had no means of knowing how many others were similarly affected but I doubt if there was a single one in the whole brigade who didn't instinctively pull his head down and hunch his shoulders at any noise which vaguely resembled an incoming mortar bomb. Even as we lay there, one of the biggest chaps in the Commando, over six feet tall and as broad as a barn door, tottered past. He was moving like an automaton, arms partly outstretched to maintain balance, every halting step an obvious effort. His head lolled from side to side, and his eyes, just like Bill's, were staring straight ahead, blank and apparently unseeing. He was alone, and at first I wondered why none of his pals was helping him, then I guessed that he probably still had sufficient grasp of the situation to tell them to 'F... off! I can look after myself' – and he was a very big fellow.

Towards evening, when conditions had quietened down, I was given the job of taking Bill back to the Commando RAP (Regimental Aid Post), the first stage down the medical line for all battle casualties. Each unit had their own medical men (in the case of the Royal Marines these went under the naval term 'sick-berth attendants' – SBAs) who set up an aid post as close to the front line as possible. There the wounded were patched up, usually with no more than field dressings but sufficiently well to enable them to be moved on to the next stage down the line to the rear area's, Advanced Dressing Station (ADS), where more sophisticated dressings would be applied before moving the casualty further along his journey to a military hospital.

Slinging my rifle over my shoulder (Bill's, together with his ammunition, was left behind), we started off down the hill. No one was able to tell me where the aid post was likely to be, only that it was 'back' – somewhere. It would be merely a case of hoping for the best and looking out for the RAP sign. Bill was much calmer now that conditions were quieter; the moaning and twitching had subsided but he was still in a complete daze. His movements were jerky, he was unsteady on his feet and hung heavily on my arm as we tramped down the hillside.

We reached the doorway in the wall that had been used on the first day ashore without having found the Commando RAP. I lead him out onto the roadway, heading down towards Vietri. After only a few hundred yards we came across an Army aid post in a small, dark barn. The medics were very sympathetic but protested that there was nothing they could do for Bill. He would have to be passed back to the ADS and, as they didn't have any transport, he would have to walk – so I might just as well take him myself, since it was only a mile down the road.

Uncomprehending and uncomplaining, Bill trudged on by my side until we reached the ADS, set up in what appeared to be a small hotel. There they accepted him but with obvious reluctance when it was realized that he had no holes in his skin. My part in Bill's journey was finished. I gave him a pat on the back, saying that it wouldn't be long before he was back with the Commando again, but he just stood there, swaying slightly and twitching involuntarily. He was lost in a world of his own, completely unaware of my identity and of everything else around him.* I turned and left, to get back up the hill.

* Bill Marshall recovered and rejoined the unit; he was badly wounded at Walcheren.

Retracing my steps up the road, in the deepening dusk, I found no problem in locating the door in the wall and started up the track we had trudged along with the machine-gun ammunition on the first day. Under the trees, however, it was almost completely black and after about half an hour I came upon an unfamiliar farmhouse and realized that I had lost my way. A cautious approach to the building revealed that, in addition to a number of Italian civilians – presumably the residents, there was also about a dozen assorted British servicemen who were obviously intending to stay there for the night. None of them could offer any help as to how I might find the Commando, and I gained a strong impression that their sole concern was to keep out of the way. Having no inclination to wander about on that hill in the darkness – with the possibility of ending up like '*Sechzig Kompanie*', I decided to join them and passed an uneasy and uncomfortable night on the crowded stone floor of the farmhouse kitchen.

Early in the morning, after scrounging a little food, I continued up the hill and came upon the Commando sitting around in groups, waiting to march back down to Vietri. Most of us were still more than a little bomb-happy and reacted instinctively to any kind of swishing sound that vaguely resembled an incoming mortar bomb. Brushing against the leaves of a tree was enough to hunch a few pairs of shoulders, while the rustle of an anti-gas cape caused automatic ducking over a wide area. Apart from such false alarms there were no other warlike noises on the hill that morning. Before we started off, Captain Wilkinson gave us a short 'Jolly good show, chaps' sort of talk and was astonished to receive a spontaneous, if very unmilitary, round of applause as we expressed our appreciation of his calm moral support on the previous day.

Once more we tramped back down the seaward slope of the hill and in due course were fallen out in a field abutting the landward side of the coastal road, with a good view of the camouflaged railway viaduct.

11 *Pigoletti*

It was now the afternoon of Tuesday 14 September, our sixth day ashore, and for the second time we revelled in a wash and shave. Then we had time to sit around in the warm sunshine to speculate upon what had gone wrong with the main landings.

The Fifth Army was evidently still heavily engaged to the south of Salerno, although the coastal strip between them and us appeared to be in Allied hands – if the Army units who had relieved us on the hill had in fact come from there. But at the same time there was no sign of any great body of troops having come forward to surge through La Molina towards the plain of Naples. Even from a marine's-eye view it was obvious that this invasion wasn't making much headway. It was even being bruited about that the ships we could see lying close inshore hundreds of feet below us were standing by to carry out an evacuation, should an Italian 'Dunkirk' become necessary. At the same time we knew that the Eighth Army, pushing its way up towards Salerno, wasn't very far away and hoped that we would still be around when they made contact with the Fifth.

It was many years before I learned that the previous day, 13 September, had been 'Black Monday' for the Salerno operation. The possibility of an evacuation had been all too real and figured large in the contingency plans of General Mark Clark, although it seems that most, if not all, of the other senior commanders had no such ideas. The night I had spent in that Italian farmhouse had been the crucial period of the whole invasion. At the junction of the Sele and Calore rivers, the boundary between the

British and American divisions, hard pressed in the main beachhead, only a few hundred men and a dozen or so guns stood between the Germans and the sea. If there had been a breakthrough, it would have split the invasion forces in half, and that could, perhaps, have precipitated an evacuation – but the enemy hadn't made the push, and the gap had been plugged early next day.

It also became known that the situation of the Commando Brigade on Black Monday had been judged by General McCreery, the British Commander, to be so critical that he had sent an urgent request to Colonel Darby asking that the Rangers come to our assistance – and a battalion of them had arrived in the neighbourhood of Vietri that same evening. By then, things had been stabilized, so the Rangers returned to their own area without having been needed.

We in the Fighting Troops had known nothing about this, nor had we even been aware of the continuing liaison between the American and British Special Forces on the Sorrento peninsula. The viaduct we had crossed on that first night ashore had featured prominently in those contacts, as it provided the only vehicular link between Maiori and Vietri sul Mare. The American Ranger officer who made most of the liaison trips had christened it 'The how's-about-it-now bridge'. It was under direct observation by the Germans, who invariably opened fire on any vehicle attempting to make the crossing. In the quiet periods between these outbursts of shelling, the British military police controlling traffic using the bridge would approach drivers waiting to run the gauntlet and suggest, 'How's about trying it now?'

Casualties had been very heavy throughout the Commando. All six Fighting Troops were badly under strength, and more than half our officers had been killed or wounded – Q Troop being without any at all with the confirmation of Captain Stott's death. Thus the Commando was reorganized into four understrength Fighting Troops, and P and Q ceased to exist. I was detailed off to a newly constituted B Troop with the designation of 'bren-group commander' but was allocated only two men instead of the normal three. My bren-gunner was Bill Smith, still with Betsy, and as his No. 2 he had a character called Harold Colloff.

These two were the 'old men' of the Troop. Both would have been past their mid-thirties at the time – something like fifteen years older than most of us – but they were the two best stickers of the lot. During training, no matter how gruelling the forced march, nor how few were still going at the end of it, you could be sure that Bill and Harold (somehow we never even thought of calling him 'Harry') would be amongst them. Bill was a burly, round-faced glassworker from St Helens, Lancashire, with a wry sense of humour, but I suspect he wasn't entirely joking when he said he was undecided about what to do after the war – whether to get married or to buy a couple of greyhounds. I never did learn the answer to that one, nor whether he got the job in the continuous rolling mill at Pilkingtons glassworks which he hoped for. Harold was a short, stocky compositor from Manchester, who invariably wore his hair cropped very short and always started to read a newspaper at the financial page, to check on his investments. It would have been impossible for me to have chosen a better pair.

All the same, I wasn't at all overjoyed at the appointment. The job undoubtedly carried some additional responsibility (without any extra pay), and I had been in the marines long enough to realize that I would have to spend much of my time humping the gun – which weighed twenty-three pounds, 2½ times as much as a Lee Enfield rifle.

The local inhabitants were more numerous on Tuesday afternoon than they had been on Sunday morning, and there were frequent comings and goings along the road outside the camp. Children from the age of not much more than two years had quickly learned the chant of 'Cigarette for papa!' which had been part of our everyday life in Sicily. But we were much too short of cigarettes for ourselves to act as benefactors to doubtful Italian fathers, who should have been away in the armed forces anyhow. Nor were we in a position to respond to the Italian mothers, who came along in person and in great numbers to wail, *'Molti bambini – niente mangiare'*. The thought of 'many children' with 'nothing to eat' was naturally rather depressing – they had our sympathy but they didn't get our food. There was, in fact, little enough for ourselves; we were already on short rations, and unfilled British bellies were starting to give rumbles of hunger. That night, before curling up to sleep on the bare ground, we had another session of searching through pockets and pouches for any last crumbs of biscuit or chocolate that might previously have been overlooked.

Breakfast next morning wasn't very substantial either. Each man received one sausage, compo, tinned, two biscuits and a two-ounce bar of chocolate. Not much food, but it was much more palatable than the instructions issued with it:

'Don't start any dhobying after breakfast. We'll be moving off during the morning.'

'Not up that fricking hill again?' was our immediate reaction.

But no – it was like Mohammed and the mountain: the Fifth Army was unable to come up to us, so we were to go down to join them. Despite the direction of our move, it was at least a pleasant surprise to find that transport had been laid on. We climbed up into the TCVs with a mixture of curiosity (to see some more of Italy) and apprehension (about what might lie in store for us this time). The trucks rolled off towards Salerno, and in no time at all we were bowling along wide city streets flanked with tall, substantial buildings, all apparently undamaged. The place was dead and completely empty – we were the only moving things disturbing the all-pervading silence.

The countryside beyond the town was equally deserted, although there was little time to appreciate it as our ride ended after only two or three miles. We debussed and continued on foot, along a narrow, grassy cart track. For another mile or two we sweated under the midday sun before being directed through a gate set in a high hedge on the left-hand side of the track. We found ourselves in a secluded orchard on one of the lower slopes of some more of those Italian hills and were told that the Commando was being held in reserve, so we should get started on digging our sleeping-quarters. It was then about one o'clock in the afternoon but instead of lunch we received an assurance that a ration truck was on its way to us.

The ground was as hard and as stony as any we had encountered but at least there was a respectable depth of soil. The afternoon was well advanced by the time we had finished our excavations. All the time we had been working, the countryside remained calm and serenely peaceful without the sight of any other living creature or any sound of war. By then we were rather weary after our exertions, hotter than ever and, as the promised ration truck still had not arrived, so much more hungry. Nevertheless, as we stretched out under the squat, bushy trees for a stand-easy, there was an air of relaxed contentment in that well-dug orchard. We had finished our stint of digging for the day and had a pleasant, quiet resting-place for the night. We stretched out full length on the ground, using the soil from our holes as pillows. Tired eyelids dropped shut, blotting out those patches of blue sky, with just a few wispy white clouds floating by, which had been visible through the branches of the trees. The drowsy heat, together with the melodious buzzings of myriads of flying insects, lulled many into a dozing torpor.

'All right! Wakey! Wakey! Wakey! On your feet! Get rigged! We're moving off!'

The raucous voice of our new Troop sergeant jerked us back into a reluctant consciousness. We stumbled to our feet, blinking sleepily while struggling to collect scattered wits and equipment. Now the buzzing in the previously peaceful orchard was very much louder – not with flying creatures but with questions, conjecture and bad language. We buckled on our webbing, hitched packs into position and draped around our necks the bandolier of fifty extra cartridges which we had been required to carry on this occasion. Steel helmets and weapons clutched in our hands, we gathered around the sergeant, expecting to learn what it was all about, but he had no other information than that we were to be formed up ready to move off immediately the troop commander returned from his O Group with the commanding officer. We got fell in.

The captain appeared a few minutes later to give us a brief synopsis of the situation – simply that the Germans had recaptured a hill which General Mark Clark badly needed, so we were to get over there without delay and get it back for him. There would be tank support but that would be explained to us when we were briefed for the attack, at the jumping-off point, a few miles away. Time was short, so the approach march was to start immediately. As soon as the officer had finished speaking, the sergeant took over again and, rank by rank, we stumbled off through the trees to tag onto the long snake of the Commando already trooping out of the orchard.

It was a subdued and seemingly miserable string of men that filed through the gate, turned left onto the uneven track and headed towards the hills at a quick march. Maybe the innermost feelings of the others were different from my own but I recall experiencing an abject sense of dejection that had never been there before. Neither prior to either of the landings nor on the hill at Vietri had there been such a dull emptiness in the pit of my stomach – and it had absolutely nothing to do with a meagre breakfast followed by a non-existent lunch and no tea. Perhaps the others were simply just too browned off to speak but it was noticeable that there was none of the usual cross-talk and banter which usually helped to take your mind off the monotony of putting one foot in front of the other, *ad infinitum*.

The whole column trudged along in absolute silence; even the 'dripping' (naval slang for grumbling and grousing, which is part of many a marine's basic make-up) was absent. Each man appeared to be lost in his own thoughts, as if his nervous system required some time to adjust to the sudden and unexpected jolt from 'reserve', with the anticipation of a night's rest in a quiet orchard, into 'attack' – and at such an unusual time of the day. Back in the UK it would be getting close to the end of the working day, and my mind formulated pictures of crowded tramcars and tube trains in the evening rush-hour. Most ordinary people would soon be flocking home, intent only upon their tea and the six o'clock news from the BBC. Why the hell, I thought, should we be flogging our guts out to get to a bloody Italian hill – and then maybe get ourselves killed trying to chase a bunch of bastard Germans off it?

The track continued to climb through a well-wooded countryside, unmarked by war, silent and empty. Tramping steadily upwards, the feeling of dull, empty heaviness gradually lifted. We became resigned to having sweated all through a glorious afternoon, digging holes which we would never use, and the knowledge that there was another of those blasted hills awaiting us also became accepted. We even managed to glean some comfort from the fact that, for the time being at least, there were no mortar bombs bursting about our heads and were buoyed up by the conviction that there would surely be another issue of K rations prior to starting the business.

It was early evening by the time we reached the jumping-off point, at the foot of the hill we were required to recapture. The serpentine column of the Commando wound its way off the grassy track and onto a tarmacadam carriageway. We were gathered together in untidy groups, to hear staff officers outline the plan of attack.

On the left-hand side of the road, nestling against a hedge and hidden from the air by the overhanging branches of trees, were the tanks – four or five Shermans. Their role was to be twofold: they would provide artillery support for the attack (keeping the enemy's heads down while we approached their position), then act as an armoured shield for our final assault. A major problem was that their only possible route to the top of the hill was by way of the road on which we were standing and, when breasting the summit, they would be 'sitting ducks', exposing their soft underbellies to any anti-tank guns the Germans might have up there. To ensure that the defenders were in no position to take advantage of this, it was proposed that a substantial part of the Commando should be positioned on the top of the hill before the tanks arrived – to make certain that the German anti-tank gunners were more concerned about keeping their heads down than firing their weapons. Once the tanks were on the top of the hill, which we were told was relatively flat, they would deploy into extended line and advance upon the enemy with guns blazing while shielding us from small-arms fire as we tagged along behind until close enough to make a bayonet charge. Part of the Commando was to ride up on the tanks to deal with any enemy infantry that might be encountered *en route*. Just before reaching the top, these riders would hop off and join the rest of the Commando for the final assault. B Troop would be with those who were to climb the hill in advance of the tanks.

While our ears and brains were absorbing this information, all eyes had been searching around, almost desperately, for anything that might indicate the presence of food. But there was no sign of a ration truck, no stockpile of boxes of 'Ks' – nothing. The subject wasn't even mentioned. It was evident that we would just have to carry on being hungry.

Then we became even less impressed with the proposed operation when the officer went on to explain that, in the absence of any artillery unit in the area, the tanks had already given the hill a preliminary bombardment. We looked at one another with the shaking heads of questioning incredulity. There had been absolutely no sound of gunfire during the approach march, and we knew enough about being under fire to be more than a little sceptical about the effect upon well-dug-in troops of the 75mm guns of a few Sherman tanks – especially if this had been carried out during some unspecified period in the past. However, ours was not to reason why, and the time had already come for the foot-sloggers to start slogging. With a barrage of envious catcalls and none-too-polite gestures at the lucky riders, who were already gleefully clambering on board their vehicles, we crossed over to the right-hand side of the road and began to climb the terraced hillside. Soon we heard the tanks rumbling off to their forward position, to await our arrival at some pre-arranged rendezvous, before continuing their journey to the top.

Two yards up, then five yards along; two yards up, then five yards along. Once again we were ascending the giant's staircase. The heights of the risers varied but it was the same 'make a step and heave' procedure we had had to use on our second climb up La Molina. Once again it was pretty hard going, and the business seemed to be taking much longer than expected. Daylight was fading before we were anywhere near the top. As for the tanks, we had no further sight or sound of them – they were never referred to again. We just carried on following the man in front, helping him and the man behind, until there were no more terraces to climb. After that we continued moving forward along the shadowy summit of the hill, puzzled but relieved to find that the Germans had disappeared as completely as the Shermans.

B Troop continued to advance, well below the skyline to the left of the ridge. Presumably others of the Commando were doing the same on the other side of the hill. By this time we were completely out of the picture, not knowing where we were going or why. It was simply a matter of creeping forward, stopping, waiting, then creeping forward again as orders were passed down the line. With the gathering gloom, these came in ever more hushed whispers. Even after complete darkness had enshrouded the hill, we still continued to move, stop and wait, intermittently. Eventually we came upon a group of farm buildings which could be seen to have been blasted by shellfire. This, we were told, was where we would stay the night. I was directed to take my bren-group a little further down the hill, the precise position being indicated by the sergeant, whispering in the darkness, 'Right, we'd better have the bren about here.' We guessed that the Commando was taking up the usual all-round defensive position with the farm buildings as its focal point.

In complete silence Bill set up the bren while Harold and I flopped down beside him. We had no idea where we were and weren't very much concerned: for the time being it was sufficient just to have stopped. A long time later it transpired that we had been close to the village of Pigoletti. The higher echelons probably knew this at the time but they did not appear to have much information as to the whereabouts of the Germans.

The sergeant moved amongst us, warning, in a hushed voice, 'No smoking and no digging.' It looked very much as though it would also be 'No eating' until a clearly audible stage whisper came out of the darkness, 'Hey, sarge! How about some bloody grub?' None of us expected that this heart-cry of a hungry stomach would do any good but after a short while the sergeant came around again: 'OK, lads, you can open your emergency rations.'

Most of us had forgotten that we had always carried a flat tin, similar to those used for sardines, in a special pocket of our battledress trousers. Like the field dressing in another pocket, it was just part of the gear you always carried around without realizing that it was there. Apart from having been told that it was 'emergency rations', we hadn't the faintest notion what the tin might contain – and it took quite a struggle to find out. In the darkness it was no easy matter to cut a way in with our jack-knives, but with perseverance we at last managed to extract a block of a chocolate-like substance. Almost drooling at the mouth, I set to with the firm intention of devouring the lot at one go. But as soon as my teeth made contact, it became clear that we would have to work for our suppers. The stuff was rock-hard and completely unbiteable. The best that could be managed, with a lot of jaw work, was to scrape off a few tiny slivers of sustenance. The whole Commando must have been squatting around that hilltop with blocks of emergency rations clutched in their hands, gnawing away like a pack of hungry squirrels with nuts. Having finally managed to get some down into your stomach, its cloying taste very soon made you wonder whether the effort had been worthwhile after all. Most of us considered that our pangs of hunger were stayed with little more than a quarter of the block consumed. Harold, Bill and I then agreed our rota of watches for staying awake and, with one behind the gun while the other two slept on the grass alongside, we passed the remainder of what turned out to be a peaceful night.

As usual it was still dark when we were stood to next morning, with everyone awake, alert, listening and watching. Dawn came without an attack but as the sky slowly lightened we became increasingly aware of the exposed position in which we had passed the hours of darkness. Fingers itched to get hold of an entrenching tool. We were lying on a grassy track leading up to the farm buildings and, although the hillside was, in general, well covered with trees, they were rather sparse in our immediate neighbourhood and especially to our front. As daylight increased, so our field of view widened until we could see about 200 yards of grass slope falling away from us before disappearing into a sea of foliage covering the lower parts of the valley. Over the tops of these trees, half right and less than a mile away, stood another well-wooded hillside which blocked out any more distant prospect. On this opposing hill, in those parts where the trees were more widely spaced, we could see short stretches of a rough forest track snaking its way up the steep hillside from bottom left to top right. Behind us there was nothing to be seen but trees. Lying prone as we were, even the farm buildings were completely hidden from sight.

Immediately after stand-down, the Commando began digging. Everyone took turns at wielding entrenching tools and keeping a watchful eye on the open hillside to our front. We sited the bren hole a few feet forward of the track on which we had slept, where ground-level was about two feet lower. With two of us digging while the third man lay behind the gun, it wasn't long before we had a respectable trench, large enough for the three of us to squeeze into. It was none too soon. We were still putting the finishing touches to the excavation work when our ears picked up the ominous 'thump-thump-thump-thump' of a German mortar crew loosing off their first salvo of the day. Seconds later as we crouched low in the trench, sharp short 'SHH-SHH-SHH-SHHs' told us that the bombs would be landing not very far away. Then another batch and another, until conditions rapidly developed into the pattern of crouching low for the near ones, and a relieved upward glance when bombs were passing overhead to fall some distance away. I can't recall being particularly concerned about who might be getting those 'overs' but imagine that such an attitude was about normal in the circumstances.

After a while, the sharp 'craack! craack! craacks!' of German artillery fire could be heard adding their weight to the overall bombardment. The guns were obviously SPs as, from time to time, we heard the clanking of their tracks as they changed position to avoid being pinpointed by OPs (observation posts) or spotter planes. When bursts of machine-gun fire started to slash through the trees, events began to assume the pattern of those on the previous hill. On this occasion, however, there was never the same feeling of immediacy – that the Germans could be upon us in a split second. The clear stretch of hillside to our front meant that any attacking infantry would have a rough time of it before getting anywhere near our slit trench. Particularly if Betsy happened to be in a firing mood.

Our water was replenished during the morning. One of the chaps flitted around the holes collecting empty bottles and whizzed back again with them full. There were continuing promises of rations getting up to us but in the meantime we gnawed away at the blocks of emergency stuff from time to time. We soon realized, however, that the chocolate taste created a much deeper thirst than we had water to slake, so this was resorted to with less and less frequency.

Between the flurries of bombs and shells, we kept a sharp look-out for any movement down below us on our own hill and at the same time were able to watch out over the tops of the trees towards the other side of the valley.

Shortly after receiving the water, we were intrigued to see a jeep, flying a large white flag, go bouncing and skidding its way up the track on the hill opposite. We tried to put two and two together and decided that the Germans must have radioed their intention of surrendering. Perhaps the Eighth Army were already moving in behind them, and the jeep was on its way to collect their plenipotentiaries. Sure enough, after a short interval the jeep re-appeared racing downhill again and fully laden this time. Now, we thought, it wouldn't be very long before the guns and mortars were silenced. But it had all been wishful thinking. There was no let-up in the salvoes of high explosives coming in. We were forced to the conclusion that our two and two had made five. The white flag must have been a Red Cross flag, not sufficiently unfurled for us to see it properly. The jeep could only have been picking up wounded. This left us completely confused as to where the Germans actually were – or the British for that matter. The only certainties remaining were that all the shells and bombs falling on the hilltop were 'anti-us' and that those arriving with a very short 'SSSHHH' were much too close for comfort.

Around midday we received an issue of cigarettes and a further assurance that there would soon be some real food. The mortaring continued intermittently but it now seemed as though most of the small-arms fire was being directed towards the other side of the hill beyond the farm buildings, where we heard that other Troops of the Commando were suffering casualties. In our sector we heard none of those hair-raising 'brrrrrrrrrrrrps' of German Schmeissers, and it began to seem likely that the streams of bullets which still whistled around our heads from time to time were from long-range machine-guns.

The afternoon wore on without any great change. Conditions on our part of the hill remained generally noisy and unpleasant. Our only real knowledge of the situation was negative but welcome – none of the half-dozen or so chaps visible from the bren-gun hole was hit. Throughout the day we saw nothing that looked like a German, and Betsy was never called upon to demonstrate her prowess. As the afternoon slipped into evening, we were disturbed less and less; as the shadows lengthened with the dusk, all noise of battle died away completely. It had been a long, cramped day, without any understanding of the overall situation, but we could at least draw satisfaction from the fact that the Commando was still in possession of the hill, as we had clearly been in some kind of defensive position. It transpired later that on that day the Commando Brigade had been largely responsible for repulsing a determined German counter-attack in the Pigoletti sector. Our immediate concern that evening, however, remained unchanged – when would we get some real food? By this time we were all heartily sick of the emergency ration and felt hungry in spite of it.

The last rays of the sun had long since gone when, through the hushed darkness, the unmistakable skirl of the bagpipes floated across from the general direction of the other hill. 'The Highland Division'! – the magic words flashed through our minds. We knew that those 'ladies from hell' – as the Germans had called the kilted Scots during the First World War – were part of the Eighth Army and assumed that they were, even then, pushing their way towards us. They must be almost here! I entertained visions of the doughty Scotsmen, marching three abreast through the Italian hills, kilts swirling to the rhythm of the pibroch, with all the Germans within earshot disappearing rapidly in a northerly direction.

It was soon realized, however, that there was only one piper and that the sound, initially not so very far away, had moved no closer. Even the tune he was playing, 'Will ye no come back again?', didn't quite fit in with the sort of occasion being visualized. Then the source of the music dawned upon us – it had all been no more than a (bag)pipe dream. We were listening to Lieutenant-Colonel 'Mad Jack' Churchill, commanding officer of No. 2 Commando, who took his pipes everywhere he went. Colonel Churchill was renowned for playing them in the most unlikely and unhealthy situations, generally at great personal risk to himself. He had earned his nickname in December 1941 when, as second-in-command of No. 3 Commando during the Vaagsö raid on Norway, he had stood erect in the leading landing-craft as it splashed its way to the shore, playing 'The March of the Cameron Men'. Up in the hills near Salerno, as I learned later, he was giving a solo performance while marching up and down the street outside his headquarters in Pigoletti. Maybe he had become bored and his choice of tune had been an invitation to the

Germans to put in another attack.

Curiously enough, that day had been the very one on which leading elements of the Eighth Army had made contact with the Fifth. For us in the warm darkness at the time, however, it had at least been reassuring to receive confirmation that No. 2 Commando wasn't very far away. At the same time, the sound of pipes, which had played a significant part in the Commando training course, coming as it did out of the peaceful night after a long, trying day, seemed divorced from reality and flooded the mind with memories of Achnacarry. There we had awakened to the sound of the pipes and, at the end of every speed-march – when you had been moving at about six miles an hour, you were piped back to camp, for the last half mile or so, at the normal three. (Most would have much preferred to continue speed-marching all the way to the hut to flop down on their beds rather than dawdle along.) It also reminded us of Q Troop's own piper, Alec Kennedy, who had been killed only a few days previously, on that other hill.

But reveries about the bens and lochs around Fort William were suddenly swept from our minds. Word was passed around in the darkness that the Commando was required to attack yet another hill – that same night. We were gathered together in small groups to be briefed. The objective, for some reason unknown to us, was referred to as 'The Pimple'. It had previously been in Allied hands but was subsequently re-taken by the Germans. Now we were expected to reverse the situation. In essence, the actual attack was to be a two-Troop affair with a third Troop in reserve. The fourth Troop of the Commando was to ascend partway up the opposite side of the hill to that on which the attack was to be mounted and do no more than fire their weapons, creating a diversion to hold the attention of the defenders. Immediately prior to the final assault by the attacking Troops, the Pimple was to receive a very special bombardment. Every gun in the sector, on land and on the warships lying off shore, within range and capable of being brought to bear upon the target, would lay down an intensive preliminary bombardment. Then, as the remnants of the defenders were rising to meet the anticipated attack from the decoy Troop, the real assault would go in from their rear, and the hill could be given back to the Army.

B Troop had been selected for the diversionary role, and while the other three Troops were moving round to their jumping-off position on the far side of the Pimple, we would assemble on a hill just one valley away from the objective. The Troop would move off at 0200.

'Any questions?'

'Yes, sir. When do we get something to eat?'

12 *The Pimple*

It was midnight when we each received another pack of K rations – the first real food since breakfast the previous morning. At 0200 hours, when we were gathered together to move off for the attack on the Pimple, all that remained were a few biscuits and candies stuffed into bush-jacket pockets or ammunition pouches. Together with Bill and Harold, I joined a huddle of shadowy figures forming up in an overall darkness relieved only by the dim whiteness of the farm buildings. After a whispered roll-call we were on our way.

The approach march to our hilltop assembly point was no different from any other night manœuvre anywhere. Marching in single file, seeing little more than the dark shape of the man ahead, you reacted to his every movement. When he halted and sank to the ground, you stopped and crouched low; when he rose to his feet and moved off, you tagged along behind. Strict silence was mandatory except when something untoward was encountered: then the man in front would wait until you had moved up beside him and whisper 'Wire!' or 'Hole!' or whatever the obstacle or instruction was, before moving forward again, leaving you to pass the message back to the next man. The march lasted for about 1½ hours and, as we had suspected, carrying the bren-gun was left entirely to Bill, Harold and me.

At the jumping-off point, on the hill opposite the Pimple, our shadowy file halted when the track we had been following brought us into a small wood or orchard. We received the order to fall out and await the appointed time for moving across the valley, where we were to create our diversion.

In that split second, the stillness of the night was shattered by the screaming approach of shells – lots of them. Somebody yelled, 'Get down!' but we were already on the move, scattering to both sides of the track and flinging ourselves to the ground. I landed half under a bush just as the shells began to crash down around us. The dark hillside erupted into a tumult of blinding flashes and ear-jarring explosions. More and more missiles followed in a continuous torrent until the screaming swishes of their approach, the thumps as they struck the ground, and their shattering detonations combined into one hellish uproar. The nearer shellbursts hurled fragments of rock and torn earth onto our backs as we lay flattened to the ground. Whirring chunks of steel slashed through the air and lacerated the branches above our heads. A rising cloud of smoke began to envelop the entire area, and the acrid fumes of burnt cordite built up in our nostrils.

The deluge of high explosives kept on until the whole smoky inferno built up into an unbelievable nightmare. It seemed impossible to be lying there, still unscathed, if this barrage of shells was actually happening. At the same time another compartment of the brain – even though bemused by the intensity of the noise – was in no doubt that the shells were very real. Then, in a flash of enlightenment, the truth clicked home! These were 'our' shells, streaming from the muzzles of all the British guns in the area, intended for the Germans across the valley – but falling onto the wrong hill! Someone must have given the gunners the wrong map reference – the co-ordinates of our forming-up position and not those of the Pimple.

After what seemed to be an eternity, although it was probably no more than about ten minutes, the rain of shells dried up just as abruptly as it had started. We lay dazed for quite a few seconds until roused by the voice of the Troop sergeant bawling, 'B Troop, over here! Muster over here, B Troop!' I crawled out from under my bush and homed in on his voice. Indistinct shadowy figures were materializing out of the darkness to congregate around the sergeant. Eyes peered closely as more shapes joined the group; anxious voices quietly called out the names of particular friends. Harold and I found one another without much difficulty but there was no sign of Bill with the bren. The sergeant continued to call 'Over here, B Troop!' for a few more minutes until the Troop commander decided that we couldn't wait any longer and gave the order to move off.

As Harold and I were recent additions to B Troop, few of the men were well known to us, so we had no means of assessing how many casualties had been suffered. Certainly there were fewer than three dozen of us in the string of featureless shapes that moved off heading towards the Pimple. All we learned at the time was that Major Edwards, acting CO since Colonel Lumsden's injury, had been badly wounded.

We left the trees and were soon slithering and sliding down a rough, stony track, as if on a speed-march. By that time we must have been well behind schedule unless the bombardment, as well as having been put down on the wrong hill, had also been early. After about half a mile we quitted the track, turned half-left through the gateway alongside a small ruined cottage, then began to move across open grassland falling away steeply towards the deep shadows of the valley bottom. At the other side of the gloomy abyss, our objective stood out against the pale grey sky – a huge black silhouette which grew higher with every step we took.

Reaching the foot of the slope, we were soon stumbling over flat ground made rough with a pockmarking of scores of shallow bomb-craters – clearly where some troops had been subjected to a heavy bombardment. We were picking our way through an extensive orchard. There was just sufficient light to enable us to make out the damage which had been suffered by the trees in the many blasts of high explosive which had devastated the area – lacerated trunks, shattered branches and here and there a tree completely uprooted and cast flat to the ground. Passing one bare skeleton of a tree, perhaps ten feet high, it could be seen that every leaf had been stripped from its branches. Scattered around on the grass lay the fruit, like dozens of small tennis balls. 'Peaches!' – the one word passed down the line and, scarcely pausing in our stride, every man scooped up a few, pushed them into pocket or pouch and began biting and sucking, with no slowing down of the speed of march.

Nearing the foot of the Pimple, we stumbled across more evidence of the fighting that had taken place around there. Strewn over a wide area were ammunition boxes, mortar-bomb carriers, fighting-order packs, water-bottles, steel helmets and other abandoned debris of war. Here and there, no more than larger items amongst the general litter, lay the bodies of some British dead. Immediately after leaving the orchard we entered a large, sombre wood and passed within a few feet of the corpse of another soldier. It was just visible in the gloom, as a white shape sprawled against the black bankside, stripped completely naked by some freak of the explosion that had killed him.

Under the dense roof of leaves, the blackness was almost complete. We stumbled slowly upwards between tall forest trees until we came upon a rough track leading steeply in the general direction of 'up'. The column turned left to follow it, and our progress became much easier. We padded along quickly, rubber-soled boots making little noise on the hard-beaten earth. Within the wood it was dark, silent and eerie. High above us could be heard long bursts of heavy machine-gun fire which indicated that, unlike the hill we had climbed the previous evening, this one was still occupied. We marched rapidly, gaining height steadily and with no suggestion of a halt. I began to wonder just how soon we would stop to get on with our diversionary activity. We had been given no specific details of the where and when, but it had been intimated that our task would not take us much beyond the lower slopes. There, we had understood, it would be necessary only to fire our weapons at intervals to let the Germans know that somebody was active on the hill below them and so hold their attention while the two attacking Troops sneaked up the other side of the hill. I was beginning to think that it was about time to call a halt.

The blackness ahead lightened as the track took us out onto an open, grassy hillside. The machine-gun fire, which had continued intermittently all the while we had been in the wood, could now be seen as fiery strings of tracer bullets streaming back in the general direction of the hill we had recently left. Moving out of the containment of the trees also brought us within earshot of the enemy. Guttural German voices floated down from the indistinct darkness of the upper slopes. We couldn't understand what was being said but what was even more incomprehensible was the fact that we could hear voices at all. For us a night manoeuvre of any description meant the absolute minimum of noise, and woe betide any man who infringed, but those Germans were calling to each other as though ordering last rounds in a crowded pub on Saturday night.

The sky had grown appreciably lighter by this time, and after a few hundred yards, in the half light on the open slope, we were relieved to move into the concealing shadows of another wooded area, although the trees were very much smaller and more widely spaced. Now we abandoned the gradual rise of the track and headed straight for the top. Minutes later a burst of automatic fire swept over our heads. It was close enough to suggest that the Germans realized that something was happening on the slopes below them, but far enough away for us to guess that they couldn't see anything. The climb continued and the firing stopped.

Daylight was very close; we could make out each other's faces for the first time but, because of the trees and the uneven slope of the hillside, could distinguish only the two or three men immediately ahead and perhaps one or two behind. With the improving visibility we increased the distance between men but still kept on in a straggling single file, struggling up the hillside. Another stream of bullets zipped over our heads, but much closer this time. The chaps in front of me hugged the ground, and I was happy to follow suit, wondering if at last we would start our diverting business. But no, an urgent call from above –

in English this time – got us moving again. 'Come on!' shouted the sergeant. 'Don't loaf around down there!' We pushed ourselves away from the comforting hillside and pressed on.

For some minutes more we climbed steadily, clutching at tufts of the long, coarse grass to help us negotiate the steeper stretches. Our eyes were continually searching the hillside above, and to our flanks for any sign of Germans. One more long burst of machine-gun fire, then the whole hill seemed to fall into a pregnant silence; even the German voices were stilled. Had the defenders just lost sight of us or was it, perhaps, only a case of 'Will you step into my parlour?'

It was almost full daylight when we moved into extended line, spreading ourselves out along the contours of the slope, five yards between men – but still scrambling upwards and more than ever at a loss to know just what we were supposed to be doing there. No further instructions had been given but there was no doubt at all that we were getting very close to the summit – still with no suggestion of our climb coming to an end. The hillside now was largely open grass with only a few random trees. The gradient too was changing, easing off into a gradual slope which disappeared over a low brow only a short distance ahead of us. Breasting the summit of this hump, there was just enough time to see that we had come upon a stretch of flat-looking country, well covered with low, prickly bushes, beyond which was a jumble of more trees with a background of some higher ground. At that point the Germans opened fire in earnest.

The area was sprayed with small-arms fire, and simultaneously, mortar bombs started to swish down amongst us. Instinctively we threw ourselves flat and crawled rapidly forward to the cover of the nearest bushes. This took us into a shallow depression, an area of 'dead ground', below the line of fire of the machine-guns. But not before a number of the Troop had been hit. Two of the more seriously wounded were dragged to the scant protection of a large tree and given morphia. Mortar bombs continued to fall and, with machine-gunners just waiting for us to show ourselves, there was clearly no future in pushing forward at that point. The officer sent a sergeant with two marines to probe around to our left flank to see if there was any possibility of making forward progress in that direction.

The patrol crawled away; the rest of us kept our heads down and waited. We were reasonably safe from the machine-guns, so long as we stayed flattened close to the ground, but there was no protection from the bombs. Another chap was wounded and moaned with pain until a sick-berth attendant crawled across and gave him a shot of morphia. Then a clump of bushes about twenty yards away was set alight by a bursting bomb, and the crackle of the fire was added to the general cacophony. As the smoke from the conflagration drifted up into the still morning air, it began to look as though it was only a question of time before we were either blasted out of our position or smoked out. The sun was now above the trees, adding its warmth to that of our general situation. After about ten minutes the patrol returned, to report, 'No joy.' The concealing clumps of bushes in which we were lying soon petered out, and beyond them lay a stretch of open hillside. There was no point in staying where we were. The officer signalled us to pull back the way we had come.

Cat-crawling flat on our stomachs for about forty yards took us back over the brow; then we squirmed down to the steeper part of the hill where we were hidden from the sight of the Germans. Told to move to the left, we rose to our feet and, still crouching very low, ran pell-mell along the hillside. After about 200 yards the grass slope merged into cultivation terraces. We ran along one of these for another few hundred yards and were then ordered to make for the top again.

I had been running alongside Harold, and we now found ourselves moving in company with the Troop officer and sergeant. The four of us climbed up from terrace to terrace until, squirming over the lip of another riser, we could see that there was nothing above the next one but open blue sky: we had reached the topmost terrace. We scampered quickly across to the protection of a seven-foot-high wall of earth cut into the hillside. Leaning against it, sweating profusely and breathing heavily, we saw the officer look at the sergeant and, with an upwards inclination of his head, mutter, 'Better have somebody up there.'

Harold and I didn't need to be told who was going to be 'it', so we didn't wait. Propping our rifles against the earth face, we kicked footholds in the soil and, grasping the edge of the terrace wall, hauled ourselves slowly upwards to peer circumspectly over the top. There was little to be seen – only about five yards of gently rising grass slope, then lots and lots of sky where the grass disappeared from sight over a hump in the ground. We dropped down again and, as Harold was the smaller, I made a step for him, then heaved up – he slithered quickly over the top. After I had passed up our rifles, he grasped my hand and helped me scramble up alongside him. Side by side, rifles at the ready, we eased ourselves up the grassy slope until we could peer over the brow.

Before us, indeed, lay the summit of the hill. It extended for some hundreds of yards in most directions, although much of it was hidden from our view by trees and hedges. So far as could be determined, it was reasonably flat apart from one menacing exception. Little more than 400 yards away, 'half-left' from where we lay sprawled on the ground, a bush-covered hillock thrust its head to a height of some fifty or sixty feet above the general hilltop level. It stood out from the otherwise flat terrain, just like a ... of course! ... a pimple! There presumably was the origin of the name given to the Commando objective. Some pimple! It dominated the whole hilltop area and had undoubtedly been the vantage-point from which the machine-gunners had fired upon us on our first reaching the top.

The bank on which we found ourselves was just a small clearing of bare grass, a fifteen-yard gap in the trees and bushes that fringed the top edge of the hill. To our front it gave us no cover whatsoever, apart from that provided by the slope of the ground itself, and the fact that this disappeared from view only a dozen feet or so away from us was disconcerting in the extreme. It meant that immediately to our front lay an area of dead ground, completely hidden from sight, which would provide the Germans with a safe, unseen route of approach to within three or four yards of where we were lying – out in the open, under the now broiling sun.

It needed only a swift glance to absorb this whole panorama and its major implications, but our immediate attention was riveted upon a group of three Germans moving through the bushes on the Pimple. They were about half way up, weighted down with guns or ammunition, and heading towards the top. Harold and I exchanged glances before opening rapid fire. If only Bill was here with Betsy! Almost simultaneously, as if in response to our thought, the laboured stutter of a bren joined in our firing, from a point which sounded to be some thirty or forty yards to our right – at least we now knew that we were not quite alone at the top of the hill. All visible movement on the Pimple ceased abruptly.

This bit of offensive action had given some satisfaction, but we realized that it had also alerted the Germans and revealed our approximate whereabouts. The machine-guns on the hill opened fire again – and in our general direction. They had an appreciable height advantage, so we had to be extremely careful not to raise our heads too far. This forced us to ease back a little way down the slope and concentrate our attention on an area of lightly wooded parkland to our right front, which we could still keep under observation with our heads below the line of fire from the Pimple. Unfortunately the foliage of the trees reduced the field of view, and there were a number of hedges which would provide good cover for the other side. One line of hedgerow was a particular hazard: it ran obliquely towards the edge of the hill, masking our view over a wide area of the hilltop and terminating in another patch of dead ground which, we realized, must have been very close to the spot where we had judged the bren to be sited. This combination of topography and vegetation made our position extremely precarious.

Harold and I could only assume that there were others of B Troop, like ourselves and the bren-gunner, strung out along the rim of the hilltop plateau, but just how many there were and where they might be located we had no way of knowing. Apart from each other, we couldn't see any of the Troop, and all we knew for certain was that the Troop commander and sergeant were down on the terrace below us. Enemy mortars resumed their work, and conditions became rather sticky. For about half an hour it seemed as though the Germans were content to continue machine-gunning and mortaring, and once again their bombs ignited a clump of bushes – some fifteen yards to our right. The crackling fire sent a column of white smoke curling sluggishly into the breathless morning air.

At about this stage the Troop commander was joined by his signaller, still trying, unsuccessfully, as he had throughout the ascent of the hill, to make contact with Commando Headquarters on his '18 set'. This was finally abandoned and 'Sigs' was ordered to send a morse message using his whistle. I caught sight of him a minute or two later, standing on the edge of a terrace, some two or three below us, blowing what must have been a completely ineffectual string of dots and dashes over the tree-tops. After only a minute or so this must have sounded as pathetic to the Troop commander as it did to us: we heard the signaller being told to forget the whistle and take the message, whatever it was, back to HQ on foot. Considering the length of time it had taken us to reach the hill, then climb to the top, and taking into account the strong probability that the Germans were even at that moment moving in for the kill, Harold and I had no illusions about any possible effect that that message could have upon our immediate future.

It was swelteringly hot lying there in the open, under the blazing sun, watching and waiting for the German infantry to move in. The water in our bottles was almost finished, so we had to ration ourselves to infrequent sips to moisten parched lips and lubricate dry throats. The signaller had not been gone very long when the mortaring and machine-gun fire died away and we began to catch fleeting signs of movement through the trees and along the other side of the hedge to our right front. We fired at them all, but with more hope than conviction. The bren-gun was now firing almost non-stop, and I wondered how many times the No. 2 had called out, 'Tenth magazine – barrel!' From the general upsurge of activity in that direction, it was clear that the first infantry attack was being aimed at the bren. There were positive signs of Germans advancing along the other side of the hedgerow. Blurred shapes flitted past the less dense stretches, and here and there could be seen the movement of a disturbed branch. Harold and I were firing almost continuously. Once we saw the black shape of a hand-grenade curve up in a wide arc high above the hedge top, and I poured round after round into the estimated position of the thrower.

By this time, although the mortars had ceased firing as they could not plaster us without endangering their own men, there were still sporadic explosions banging off along the edge of the hill as hand-grenades were exchanged. The noisy chatter of machine-guns from the Pimple had been replaced by volleys of rifle fire, the 'brrrrrrrrrrrrrpps' of Schmeissers and other light automatic weapons being discharged at very much closer quarters.

Then came the frightening realization that Germans had moved into the dead ground immediately to our front and were only feet away. We couldn't see them and they weren't shouting this time but there was no mistaking the meaning of the scufflings and the floppings about we could hear on the other side of our hump. Harold and I had had our grenades lying on the grass beside us ready for such an eventuality and now took it in turns to put down our rifles and hurl a '36' in the direction we hoped would be most effective. With all grenades gone, we lay awaiting Jerry's next move. The medley of noises – rattling and ripping bursts of small-arms fire, zipping whines of bullets and the blasting explosions of grenades – seemed to be rising to a crescendo. All of this, against a backdrop of drifting smoke and the crackling fire from the burning bushes, made us wonder if B Troop's 'diversion' wasn't fast degenerating into a 'Custer's last stand'.

Amidst the general hubbub, I imagine that Harold and I

sensed, rather than heard, the faint 'plump' of a hand-grenade landing behind us. I glanced back over my shoulder just in time to gain a split-second impression of something small, black and oval lying between our ankles before it exploded in a flash of light a puff of smoke. I felt a blow on my right calf and heard lots of whirrings and whizzings in the air around my head, before switching my gaze across to Harold. He was looking down towards his left side, and turned towards me muttering something about '... a bit in the leg ...'.

With both hands still gripping my rifle in the firing position, I instinctively called out, 'We've been hit, sir.' The Troop commander immediately replied, 'You'd better come down then.'

Before making any move, I turned to my front again to see, precisely in line with my rifle barrel, and scarcely twelve feet from the muzzle, the head and shoulders of a German – obviously looking for the effects of his grenade. The face, framed in a coal-scuttle helmet, was square-jawed, tight-lipped and expressionless, the chin black and stubbly with unshaven whiskers.

There was time for a quick squeeze of the trigger before starting to squirm backwards towards the edge of the hill, and even as I did so, the officer's voice could be heard again, this time shouting. 'All right, boys! Let's get out of here!'

13 From Hilltop to Hospital Ship

By the time Harold and I had squirmed those few feet backwards and dropped down to the terrace below, we were completely alone. Our only thought was to escape.

We raced across, jumped down to the next one, crossed that, then down again. Out of the corner of my eye I caught a fleeting glimpse of a line of dark figures silhouetted against the bright sky as we continued to hurl ourselves down the hillside in a flurry of zipping bullets. We took the drops – six feet and more between terraces – in our stride and, even when completely hidden from the ridge, continued in headlong flight. Not until a long, slithering fall of perhaps fifteen feet, where two terraces ran together, had knocked most of the remaining breath from our lungs did we decide that the time had come to proceed at a more decorous rate. Only then, after we had paused to steady thumping hearts and take a sip from the dregs in our water-bottles, did we realize that the wounds in our legs had become rather painful.

After that we lowered ourselves from terrace to terrace but, in spite of this slowing down in our rate of progress, we reached the foot of the hill in only a fraction of the time it had taken us to ascend. It was probably less than twenty minutes from 'take-off' to finding ourselves with no more terraces to negotiate, amongst a thick jumble of trees and bushes in a completely unknown stretch of countryside. By that time our legs – Harold's left and my right – had stiffened up considerably, and instead of the straight-foward 'Let's Go!', our minds were now much more concerned about 'Where to?' I had also become aware of a sticky area of discomfort in my stern quarters, where fragments of the grenade had embedded themselves in awkward and rather painful places. A narrow, ill-defined track led through the wood, and after a short halt to finish off the last vestiges of water in our bottles, we limped off through the trees.

By great good fortune, after only a few minutes, we came upon a group of five of the original B Troop gathered around our own Corporal Buck Taylor of Q Troop, discussing the route that should be taken back to Commando HQ. One of the B Troop chaps, a big, thickset fellow, was taking no part in the discussion. He was being kept on his feet by two of his mates, an arm crooked round each of their necks. As we drew closer, we saw the reason – a deep, bloody gash in the middle of his back. The direction of march having been decided upon, we started off, with Buck in the lead. Next went the man with the back wound, being half-dragged along by his pals at a tottering stumble. Harold and I were able to hobble along without assistance, grateful at having been relieved of our rifles by the other two of B Troop, who followed along behind.

Corporal Taylor seemed to have difficulty in arriving at an acceptable compromise between his desire to get back to the unit as quickly as possible and the necessarily slow pace of the wounded. He was continually being lost to sight as he forged ahead through the trees. For my part I had no idea which way we should be heading, so it was simply a matter of limping along, hoping that we were actually moving in the right direction – and that the Commando wasn't very far away.

The sun was now swelteringly hot, our water was finished and we all had raging thirsts. It seemed to be a stroke of luck, therefore, after perhaps a mile of painful progress, to find ourselves moving along a terrace of vines. The plants were supported by wires stretched between wooden posts set into the ground, and large bunches of black grapes dangled temptingly at eye-level as we hobbled along. As Buck was still pushing forward rapidly, we couldn't risk being left behind, so, without stopping, we snatched at the fruit and crammed messy handfuls into our mouths, then, after a few quick, massive chews and sucks to extract the juice, spat out the debris of stalks, skins and pips. The meagre trickles of grape juice we obtained tasted like nectar at the time, but all too soon there were no more grapes to grab, and such benefit as we had gained was dissipated almost immediately.

Some time later we stumbled into a farmyard and asked for water, but the Italians were sullen and completely unhelpful. They argued that the well was dry and there was no water to spare. This was something that Buck knew how to handle – waving his tommy-gun very close to their noses, he soon persuaded them to change their minds. Unfortunately we drank much more than we should have and within minutes of starting off again were lathered in sweat and as thirsty as ever. It had also become much more difficult and painful for Harold and me to hobble along, as the short rest had allowed our leg muscles to stiffen up almost completely. The chap with the hole in his back was somehow managing to keep going, although by this time he was practically unconscious on his feet.

The morning was well advanced by the time we eventually reached the Commando area and found ourselves in the deserted and sun-drenched main street of a village – presumably it was Pigoletti, although we hadn't the least idea where we were. At that stage I was being helped along by one of the B Troop men, our arms around each other's shoulders. Harold, with similar assistance, was a yard or two behind, and it must have looked as though we were competing in some kind of dispirited three-legged race as we limped our way slowly down the hill. We had by this time, and without knowing where or when, lost contact with the other wounded man and the rest of the party. There were only the four of us when we reached the RAP.

The Commando's aid post had been set up in a small cottage on the right-hand side of the road; it was rather smelly but its cool darkness was a welcome change from the hot brilliance of the street outside. It appeared to contain no more than two beds and one sick-berth attendant. We thanked our helpers, who immediately went off in search of their Troop. The SBA gave us a drink of water and began his ministrations. Dealing with me first, he tore open the bloody trouser leg to get at the wound in my calf, which he cleaned and covered with a field dressing. Then I lay on my face while he lowered my pants to fix another dressing on my punctured posterior. Harold's leg was then dealt with, and after a short wait a jeep arrived to transport us to the Advanced Dressing Station.

At the ADS our wounds were inspected by a doctor and fresh dressing applied. Then we were placed on stretchers, loaded into an ambulance and delivered to the next staging-point, the Casualty Clearing Station (CCS). This we found to be an administration rather than medical centre: their concern was to record our full particulars – name, rank, number, unit, next of kin etc – before putting us into another ambulance for transfer to the Main Dressing Station.

The MDS was an Italian hospital in a town – presumably Salerno, and here our documentation was checked and our wounds were examined by another doctor and re-dressed with hospital dressings. We were both earmarked for evacuation, given a mug of tea and set down against the wall of a corridor which was bustling with the comings and goings of casualties and medical staff – there to await transport for the last leg of our journey to the beach. After a while we were carried out to an Army ambulance and were rather surprised to find that, despite the numerous casualties we had seen in the MDS, we were the only two passengers for the trip. Before moving off, however, the doors were opened again and a third stretcher was slipped onto one of the racks on the other side of the gangway. We looked across to greet our travelling companion but he was beyond any kind of conversation, being completely shrouded in an Army blanket.

After only a short journey, the doors were flung open and, despite protestations that we could very well be 'walking wounded', Harold and I were told to stay on the stretchers and were lifted out and carried to the beach. But it was a crowded, shady and unreal sort of beach we were taken to – with no view of the sea and very little of the sky. A vast expanse of sand, including dunes, hummocks and marram grass and clumps of the rough, spiky bushes we had encountered on the Pimple, had been roofed over with camouflage netting as a huge sun-awning for the hundreds of wounded awaiting evacuation. It was impossible to see the full extent of that enormous waiting-room – the more distant views were cut off by rows of medical and store tents and the unmistakable plain canvas walls of latrines. Stretchers were ranged out on the sand, rank by rank with parade-ground precision, and we were set down at the end of one ever-lengthening row. Many of those already there were Germans who, like us, had just been put in line as they arrived.

A short time later we heard the drone of approaching aircraft escalate into a jumble of aerial activity directly above our heads. The netting prevented our seeing what was happening but from the screaming engines of diving aeroplanes, the rattle of machine-guns and the thumping of cannon-fire it was obvious that something very close-by was being strafed. As each plane swooped low with guns blazing, the whole expanse of wounded men instinctively flattened to their stretchers, like a field of wind-dashed corn.

When things had quietened down again, Harold and I made an effort to get into conversation with a nearby German. He showed us photographs of his wife and two children but when, with equal pride, he produced a photograph of Hitler, we decided not to prolong the acquaintanceship.

It was rumoured that a hospital ship was expected at any time so, all through the afternoon and well into the evening, we watched expectantly for any signs of movement. Those of us who were able to hobble around occupied themselves in getting drinks or lighting cigarettes for the more seriously wounded. When darkness began to creep upon us, everyone had to resign themselves to a night on the beach, irked by the delay but appreciative of all there was to be thankful for. There had been little enough sleep during the previous night, so, despite uncomfortable throbbings of the leg and other punctured parts, it wasn't at all difficult to drop off.

Next morning was Saturday, and so a good time to start a Mediterranean cruise, but we had to wait some hours before, away in the distance, stretchers could be seen being carried off by the score; then there was a long lull before the exodus started again. This stop/start procedure continued for the rest of the morning, keeping us in suspense until our turn came and Harold and I were carried out into the brilliance of full sunlight. Only a few hundred yards off shore, gleaming brightly on a shimmering sea, looking tantalizingly cool and inviting, lay a large, white hospital ship, the SS *Oxfordshire*.

Set down near the water's edge we absorbed the whole dazzling prospect until we were loaded onto a Tank Landing Craft being used as a jumbo-sized water ambulance. The trip took only a few minutes but handling the many loaded stretchers was a long and strenuous job for the RAMC men. The most ticklish part was to transfer them from the well of the landing-craft to the foot of the ship's gangway, during which time they had to be tilted through some rather alarming angles. But it was solely the idea of easing the work of the medics, rather than any fear of being dropped into the sea, that persuaded many of us to hop across and up the gangway under our own steam. Men stood waiting to direct the stretcher-bearers and to provide any assistance required by the shuffling, limping lines of walking wounded.

I had almost reached the deck when one of the walking wounded immediately ahead started shouting, 'That's the bastard who shot us up. I'll kill the fricker!' Until then I hadn't noticed a very young and extremely acne-faced Luftwaffe pilot standing on the deck. The wounded man was lurching towards him, arms flailing, and we gleaned that the German, after doing what he was alleged to have done, had been shot down and fished out of the sea. It could have happened during the strafing we had heard the previous day – the pilot was certainly quite dry. I was now regretting having abandoned my stretcher and kept moving along.

On reaching our mess deck, Harold and I settled down gingerly on the edge of the lower bunks to which we had been directed and gawped around. We marvelled at the change of lifestyle which that short sea trip had brought about. Whisked away from the hot and grubby landlubber life we had known for more than two months, we found ourselves deposited in a cool, clinically clean shipboard wonderland of polished decks and white bulkheads. Instead of rocky holes in the ground where we had slept fully clothed, there were now bunks – with mattresses – and sheets!

More than anything else, it was the smooth, pristine whiteness of those sheets which brought home to us just how dirty and bedraggled we really were. Our khaki drill had been worn day and night for the previous nine weeks, and for four days, without wash or shave, we had crawled about on the ground and sweated in the sun. Like those of the others on the mess deck, our uniforms had been ripped open to expose wounds and were caked with blotches of dried blood. Many men were without jacket or trousers, and a few were devoid of both.

The men about us, like ourselves, had suffered only minor wounds, and we all sat around waiting to be examined by the ship's doctors. When my turn came, the grenade splinters were removed from my buttocks, and the calf wound was noted on my card as a 'clean E & E' ('Entry and Exit', as I learned later). I was re-bandaged and returned to the mess deck. The next priority was a shower of as much of one's person as was possible without affecting the newly applied dressings. The ablutions were communal, so there was no problem in making reciprocal soaping arrangements to deal with those parts which couldn't be reached in comfort. With bodies once more clean and glowing, the tattered bloody clothing looked and felt more filthy than ever but the ship had no facilities for a new issue. Then came a hot meal – served on a plate – with soft white bread. We revelled in such commonplace things before enjoying the luxury of stretching out on our bunks for a siesta.

Later in the day the ship's engines pulsed into life. We were on our way – away from Salerno – away from Italy – but, most poignantly, away from our unit. For a serviceman (and it's probably the same for women) the unit, more so perhaps during time of war, is a second family. No matter where you were sent or what was required of you, all things became bearable because they were shared with your 'mates' or 'oppos'. Any separation from your unit was like being orphaned.

Before turning in that night, Harold and I limped up to the boat deck for a farewell look at the country we were leaving. Standing by the ship's rail, gazing back at the featureless hills slipping away astern, I experienced a vague feeling of guilt at sailing away, leaving the rest of the Commando somewhere up there. Our wounds, the essential tickets for the trip, were rather trivial, and I wondered whether we had paid the full fare. Talking quietly together in the warm dusk, we agreed that, deep down inside, in some indefinable way, we 'felt better'. It wasn't simply a question of having 'shed blood for King and Country' – although that could have played its part, and it must have included some measure of personal satisfaction at having been able to do what was asked of us. There could also, perhaps, have been a sneaking feeling of pride at having been involved in what had undoubtedly been a significant military occasion. On top of everything else there was a feeling of thankfulness at having come through it with nothing more than minor wounds.

A short while later, after we had slipped between those cool white sheets, the wounds were throbbing again but the mind was content. No foxhole to crouch in that night, no guard duty, no dawn stand-to in the morning, no mortar bombs, no shells, no bullets. And tomorrow there would be unlimited water, cooked meals with soft white bread and a sea trip with cooling breezes. The *Oxfordshire* would take care of everything.

Our nine days in Italy were over.

14 *North Africa – and Back to Sicily*

The Mediterranean cruise lasted less than two days. On Monday morning we awoke to find the coast of Algeria only a few miles away. By eleven o'clock the *Oxfordshire* was tied up at Philippeville (subsequently re-named Skikda). There were no disembarkation formalities, so in a surprisingly short time the wounded were being transferred to long lines of transport already waiting on the quayside. Stretcher cases were slickly loaded into ambulances, while the walking wounded (Harold and I were now accepted as such) received helping hands to board American TCVs. As soon as it was loaded, each vehicle was driven off to take its place in a seemingly unending motorcade rolling away from the docks.

Jolting through the almost deserted town we saw very few signs of an Allied military presence, and the handful of local inhabitants abroad in the streets treated our passing with the complete indifference bred of long familiarity. The countryside beyond Philippeville was even less welcoming. We found ourselves in a barren wasteland of rolling hills, with scarcely a tree to relieve the monotony. There seemed to be an aura of silent foreboding hanging over that empty landscape which gave peaceful Algeria a much more menacing aspect than we had found in the war-torn hills around Salerno.

After about eight miles the convoy passed through the settlement of Ellarouche, and a short while later it turned off the metalled road onto a dusty earth track signposted 'No. 15 Canadian General Hospital'. The hospital proved to be a sprawling tented complex covering many acres of sun-scorched grassland. It was clearly already well filled, as the TCV stopped from time to time to distribute the new arrivals amongst the wards. I was off-loaded by myself, while Harold remained on board to be taken elsewhere.

The ward to which I was delivered was a large marquee forming the heart of an extensive canvas maze of subsidiary wards, dressing-rooms, operating-theatres and offices, all interlinked with canvas-covered walkways. I was received by a hospital orderly and conducted to the only empty bed available.

Like most of the others, I had arrived in hospital with no belongings other than the clothes I was wearing, so it was like being welcomed back to normality to be presented with a toilet bag containing soap, shaving-gear, toothbrush and paste, with the compliments of the Canadian Red Cross. The orderly helped me remove my tattered uniform, drape myself in a voluminous nightshirt and climb into bed before disappearing with my bloody khaki drill tucked under his arm.

As he departed, a purposeful nurse appeared at the far end of the marquee, bearing down in my direction. It had never occurred to me that there might be female nurses in an Army field hospital, so my mouth was probably still gaping wide, ready to receive her thermometer, when she reached my bed. My documentation must have been complete because, as soon as she had changed the dressing on the calf wound, she brusquely ordered, 'Turn over.' I was only too happy to bury my face in the pillow while she did what she had to do with my *derrière*.

Most of the other patients were Canadians who had been wounded in Sicily but there was a sprinkling of British servicemen and a solitary Arab civilian who had been injured during an air raid on the port. He must have had a pretty miserable time of it for, apart from the language barrier, it was the Mohammedan feast of Ramadan, so he wasn't permitted to eat during the hours of daylight.

The ward catered for a wide variety of wounds; no two were exactly alike, but there was one overall common denominator – plaster of Paris. Irrespective of type and location, all injuries were encased in plaster casts of varying degrees of whiteness which gave a rough indication of the length of time they had been worn. On the day after my arrival I was wheeled away to have the wounds re-dressed and be passed on to the plasterer. I had joined the club. They seemed to be unduly extravagant with the plaster. The whole of my right leg, from the top of the thigh to the sole of the foot, excluding only the toes, was encased in a damp white sheath. That was fair enough, but I did feel a little sorry for myself at having been confined to bed until it was taken off. My situation was put into its proper perspective later that day, however, when a British Army driver was brought into the ward. His truck had been blown up by a mine, and from neck to ankles he was completely encased in one immense plaster cast so that he resembled nothing so much as an Egyptian mummy, wrapped ready for the sarcophagus. He was surprisingly cheerful even though he couldn't do anything for himself, and it took two strong nurses to turn him over for a change of scenery.

The plaster-cast technique was supplemented by a 'course' of 'M & B' tablets, the then current antibiotic known to all simply by the initials of its manufacturers, May & Baker. Treatment started with a massive dose of sixteen tablets, to be washed down one after another; then this was gradually tapered off, with fewer and fewer being administered at increasingly longer intervals until, if all went well, the infection had been eradicated. The humourists averred that the only reason for the plaster was to prevent any germs escaping before they had been exterminated. But it was undoubtedly the stench of dead flesh rather than dead germs that caused some of those casts to stink the way they did. A particularly 'high' one belonged to a young British naval rating who had collected a shattered elbow by getting too close to a bridge-demolition job in Sicily. His plaster stank to high heaven, and there was usually a soggy patch under his elbow where the juices were seeping through. He reckoned they wouldn't give him a fresh one until the maggots had poked their heads out.

It was three weeks before my plaster was cut off and I could wallow in that first long, blissful scratch. Harold had been moved elsewhere but, when fresh clothes were produced, I was able to take my turn at visiting others of the Commando who were still bedfast. The initial delight of being up and about quickly subsided, to be replaced by an impatience to escape from hospital clutches altogether.

A week after being de-plastered I was transferred to a convalescent hospital at Souk Ahras, some 120 miles away. This was a permanent brick-built complex, infinitely more depressing and demoralizing than No. 15 CGH, but my incarceration there lasted only four days and it was an unmitigated relief to be discharged for 'RTU' – 'Return to Unit'.

On the morning of 22 October a truckload of cheerful Army and Navy personnel left the Souk Ahras hospital for Bône (now Annaba), a small seaport about fifty miles away. Every man hoped that this was the first leg of a journey which would take him back to the pals of his own ship or unit, but few could be certain of this. I felt reasonably confident about getting back to the 41st, for there were few Royal Marines units of its kind in that theatre of war, but many of the other men were not so happily placed. A seaman could be equally effective on any of a number of different types of ship, and the one from which he had been sent to hospital might be a thousand miles away. Army men and, more specifically infantrymen could end up in 'holding battalions' to be used as general replacements for any infantry unit requiring men. It was possible that they would never rejoin their original battalion or even get back to the same regiment.

This was the basic cause of the so-called 'Salerno Mutiny'. When volunteers from a transit camp in North Africa were shipped across to Salerno believing they were going back to their own formations, they landed in Italy to discover that they were required as replacements for the 46th and 56th Divisions, and many refused to accept the postings. This eventually resulted in courts martial for those who held out, and sentences were passed ranging from seven years penal servitude for privates to the death penalty for sergeants – with a rider to the effect that the sentences would be suspended if the men agreed to join new units, so they had no option but to accept.

Service personnel who were on the move, either away from or back to their own unit or formation, were part of that flotsam and jetsam of war known as 'Ranks in Transit'. The term embraced anyone who, for one reason or another, was being shifted from place to place. Discharges, releases, replacements, new drafts and leave parties, men going on or returning from training courses or promotion courses, defaulters heading to or from the glasshouse: all swelled the flow of detached military humanity in continuous movement in all parts of the world.

It was an uncertain and generally a depressing existence. Whilst you were actually on the move, there was at least some purpose in life and, even if you weren't overjoyed at being headed for some particular destination, there was every chance that you would at least be happy at bidding farewell to the place you were leaving.

The soul-destroying part began when movement stopped. Then you had been dumped either in some existing military establishment (which had little interest in receiving you but couldn't refuse) or in one of the many transit camps set up for the sole purpose of providing minimal food and accommodation for those who had become detached from their own little niche in the military hierarchy. In either case, there you stayed, rather like sea-borne debris cast up on a beach which might be moved further along the coast by the next high tide but could very well lie there for days and days before being reached by the sea again.

The basic occupation for a Rank in Transit was to watch the noticeboard for his name, rank and number. When it did appear, there was every chance that it was simply one of a list of men detailed off for a fatigue party or a spell of guard duty: what you really wanted to see was notification of your next move. Robert Louis Stevenson must have had Ranks in Transit in mind when he wrote,

'To travel hopefully is a better thing than to arrive.' Wherever your place of arrival, the only reason for being there was to leave again – hopefully to complete the journey back to your unit.

At Bône we debussed at the naval barracks, a 'stone frigate' named HMS *Cannae*. Our party was received by the duty officer, as one of the unavoidable trials of his life which suggested that we would not be detained any longer than necessary, but it was three days before movement orders were posted – for a trip to Bizerta in Tunisia, 120 miles further along the coast. Only when the party had paraded for departure was it revealed that the journey would not be by sea, as expected, but by road, on a tank-transporter. The huge vehicle was awaiting us, piled high with crates of NAAFI stores, well sheeted over with tarpaulins. We were directed to the top of the load, and as we filed aboard, each man received rations for three days. The transporter was manned by a crew of two, under the over-all command of a sergeant riding a motor cycle, and when we had settled down on our rather precarious platform, he gave the start-up signal and rode off, to ironic cheers, with the monster vehicle trundling along behind him.

Our new hosts advised us not to 'make gannets of ourselves' with the food, as the journey would certainly take the best part of two days and could very well extend to three if they had any mechanical trouble. The first two hours of laboriously slow, low-gear progress up steep mountain gradients confirmed that the Army knew what it was talking about. It was also clear that anyone running into trouble along that stretch of highway couldn't look for help from passing motorists – the motor bike and tank-transporter had the road to themselves. We were the only moving things in a desolate world of rock, scrub and shrivelled grass. The only change in the landscape was when we came across a burnoused Arab, squatting completely alone in that vast solitude, far from the road, seemingly without transport of any kind and blissfully oblivious of our lumbering passage.

When we stopped for stand-easy near a small Arab

village, water for the tea was put to boil on the inevitable Benghazi cooker. Our brew-up became the centre of attraction for a score or more of the locals who thronged around, brandishing thick wads of banknotes and pleading, 'Bizzness, Johnny? Bizzness, Johnny?' Ranks in Transit had little enough kit for their own use, so there was little business done. With tea finished and the Arabs still hanging around, we climbed aboard again ready to move off.

Only then did the transporter team click into action – and immediately demonstrated that they were pastmasters of the 'bizzness' business. For them it was, literally, money for old rope. A coil of rope, probably acquired at the docks at Bône, had been cut into lengths about five yards each. The driver acted as spieler, dangling the rope before the noses of potential customers, haggling for his price, then his mate handled the finances when a deal was clinched. Business proceeded briskly, with the sergeant sitting astride his motor bike, some twenty yards away, watching with apparent lack of interest. When there were no more takers, the driver climbed into the cab and started his engine. As the massive vehicle rolled slowly forward, the sergeant kick-started his bike and moved into his part of the routine. Chasing after the dispersing Arabs, he relieved as many as possible of their purchases – at pistol point if necessary – before racing after the transporter, now bouncing along the road in a cloud of dust.

Two hours later we stopped again to heat up our M & V lunch. The countryside appeared as deserted as ever, but within minutes a dozen Arab horsemen, with rifles slung across their shoulders, were grouped around us. We suspected some form of retaliation for the rope trick and felt distinctly uneasy until the sergeant elicited that they too were only interested in doing business. The parley went on all during the meal but there was no response from our now subdued transporter crew. We didn't linger, and there was a huge feeling of relief when the transporter rumbled on its way, leaving the clearly disgruntled horsemen staring enigmatically after us.

At dusk we halted for the night and prepared another

meal, after which most were content to curl up by the roadside for sleep. Some of the sailors, however, went off in search of a drink at a nearby village and returned in the early hours drunk out of their senses. One climbed on the top of the NAAFI stores under the delusion that he was at sea and had stripped down to his underclothes ready to dive overboard for a swim, before being grabbed. Another appeared with a rifle and bayonet appropriated from the transporter crew and was intent upon settling an old score with one of the petty officers – until he too was held down until he lapsed into a drunken stupor. They had been drinking arrack, the local firewater distilled from dates.

Even for Ranks in Transit, that sort of travelling was not to be sought-after, and our arrival in Bizerta next day was preferable to hopeful travel. When the transporter pulled up alongside the naval barracks, HMS *Hasdrubal*, it was a pleasure to go aboard. Two days later I boarded a real ship, HMS *Cadmus*, a minesweeper bound for Malta. We completed the voyage of some 300 miles by dusk next evening and anchored in Sliema creek for the night. Next morning we moved round the headland into Grand Harbour, which was so choked with ships and landing-craft of all sizes and types that our skipper had a major problem getting his ship tied up. A Navy truck was waiting to take us to the naval barracks at Verdala, and the routine of noticeboard-watching started again.

After two days at Verdala I was transferred to Fort Manouël, where the staff were firm believers in making good use of the free labour provided by Ranks in Transit. We spent most of our time on a variety of fatigue parties, and the nights included at least one spell of guard duty. One bright spot was being allowed to draw some back pay, but going off to spend some of it visiting the local hostelries turned out to be a depressing experience. There was no shortage of beer but there were very few mugs or glasses. Every pub was besieged by hordes of Maltese youngsters hawking empty tin cans of doubtful clean-liness. It was almost enough to drive a man back to the solace of NAAFI tea.

My stay in Fort Manouël lasted four days, ending on 3

November. I doubt if the Navy realized that that was my birthday, but I gratefully accepted their present of movement orders to join an LCI(S) bound for Sicily. It weighed anchor early in the afternoon and docked next morning at Augusta, where the Commando had been put ashore after that disastrous night on the assault ships some 3½ months earlier. The Navy had taken over what had previously been an airship station of the Italian Air Force, and the huge airship hangar provided a monumental indoor parade ground.

The Commando, I learned was now in Catania, some thirty-five miles away, but that trip had to await the availability of transport, which could not be arranged until the following morning, 5 November.

I imagine that even in Guy Fawkes' day they could have bettered sixteen days to cover 600 miles.

15 *With the Commando in Catania*

The last leg of my RTU journey, from Augusta to Catania, was accomplished in some style – in the passenger seat of a 15 cwt truck. I found that the city in November bore little resemblance to the dead and deserted place we had passed through in August. The rubble and all signs of damage had disappeared, and the streets bustled with life. Most of it was of the Allied Military variety, but here too an almost unbelievable transformation had taken place. Gone were the sweating, dusty, nondescript figures in dirty khaki drill, and in their place the city was thronged with spruce soldiers promenading around in well-pressed battledress and highly polished boots. Instead of fighting order and steel helmets, with backs bent under heavy loads of guns and ammunition, the only equipment to be seen was 'belt and anklets' – and most of that stood out stark and white in freshly applied blanco. It was 'Spit and Polish-ville' with a vengeance.

From their shoulder flashes, it could be seen that most of the troops were elements of the 51st Highland Division, and when the truck passed their Divisional Headquarters, my eyes popped wide. The entrance was flanked by a pair of tall, highly polished shellcases, and two ceremonial sentries, in immaculate battledress and white-blancoed equipment, rifles at the slope and bayonets fixed, marched their post as though it were Buckingham Palace. On reaching Commando HQ it was a relief to see that the marines were not trying to out-bull the Army. There was no suspicion of a shellcase, and the webbing of our single sentry was well-scrubbed rather than blancoed. His smartness was, however, as impeccable as that of the Highlanders, if not so ostentatious.

The unit had established itself in a girls' convent school – presumably devoid of pupils at the time, as I never saw any, though a number of nuns were still in residence, and their black-habited figures could occasionally be seen pattering along the corridors or flitting across the quadrangle. More often than not they were accompanied by one or two of our young officers, but whether this was a coincidence, a courtesy or a planned escort system I never attempted to find out.

We slept on the highly polished *terrazzo* floor of a large assembly hall, in four long, orderly rows – one against each wall and two lying head to head down the centre line. With only one blanket to serve as mattress, underblanket and top covering, our beds were cold and unyielding. On the dust and dirt of Mother Earth, it was at least possible to scoop out a depression for the hip bone. The cloisters had been adapted as an *al fresco* dining-area by furnishing them with trestle tables and wooden forms. Rations were still the ubiquitous compo, but supplemented with such delicacies as bread, dehydrated potatoes and rice.

There were many new faces throughout the Commando, replacements for the Salerno casualties, but enough of the old hands remained to welcome me home. Q Troop had been reconstituted but, with all new officers and many new men, it was barely recognizable. Harold was back, and so was Bill Smith – still with his bren-gun. He too had come unscathed through the artillery barrage prior to the Pimple operation but had lost contact with the Troop afterwards. Throughout the night he had wandered about the hillside, alone and disconsolate, carrying his bren-gun which we could perhaps have put to some good use.

The Commando had been withdrawn from Italy only a day or so after the Pimple business. On their return to Sicily they had spent a few days swimming and sunning themselves near Messina before returning to our starting-point at Aci Castello. Later they had been moved to Catania. At the time of my return, the Commando was still without a commanding officer, well below strength and unsure of its future. In view of this general uncertainty, the convent was seething with buzzes about what was likely to happen next. The great majority prophesied an imminent departure – but almost every buzz-monger had us lined up for a different destination. The hottest rumour, and the one that we all wanted to believe, was that we were on the top line for a return to the UK to be re-formed and re-equipped for the 'Second Front', in Europe.

The whole city had been geared up to lure the Allied military lire from the pockets of the occupation troops, and the Italians appeared to be doing very well out of it. Ice-cream parlours, displaying their *cassata* and bewildering selections of other types of *gelati*, were particularly flourishing. Cafés advertised 'Real English Tea' and 'Genuine Canadian coffee' and there was no doubt that both claims were completely true – they had originated as official rations for the troops who were now being asked to pay good money for them. For some of the English the blow was softened, perhaps, by having the tea served amongst the potted palms and marble columns of a genuine palm court, to the accompaniment of a five-piece orchestra.

Laundry businesses were booming in a big way. Local ladies solicited customers by pushing printed cards into our hands. 'Washing – Ironing – Cleaning', proclaimed a typical example. 'Very careful service and moderate prices. Laundry collected and delivered at home billet'. The laundresses were invariably as good as their word and were well patronized by those with little aptitude for dhobying or a surplus of lire. Photographers were doing a brisk trade in studio portraits to send back to the folks at home – 'Me, in my khaki drill'.

According to the current local British Forces' newspaper, *The Eighth Army News*, organized entertainment for Allied Troops had first become available in Catania on 23 August. It had then been proud to announce that the first film to be shown at the Odeon cinema was *The Fleet's*

In, starring Ginger Rogers and Fred Astaire. That was still being shown in November, so it must have been an extremely popular choice – unless they had no other American films dubbed into Italian with English sub-titles. The Garrison Theatre appeared to be a much more popular place of entertainment, judging by the enormous queues which invariably formed outside the door some hours before the start of every performance. So long were they that I never ventured to join. On one occasion, however, I did manage to gain admission to a concert of light music played by an Italian orchestra. It was a pleasant programme of internationally appreciated favourites – until the first unmistakable bars of 'Lili Marlene' floated up from the stage and permeated the hushed and expectant audience. Naïvely, I thought that, in playing the theme song of the Afrika Korps – until recently their allies, the Italians were cocking a snook at the Eighth Army. I sat back waiting for the riot to break out – and it did, but not for the reason I had expected, and not until the last strains of the music had died away. Then the audience exploded into a tumultuous outburst of applause until the entire auditorium reverberated with piercing whistles, the prolonged stamping of heavy Army boots and continuing bellows of 'Encore! Encore! Encore!' The orchestra was obliged to give a repeat performance and would probably have had to go on doing so if they had not immediately followed on with 'God Save the King', which brought everyone to their feet and terminated the performance. No other song has ever been so completely appropriated from an enemy in the field as was 'Lili Marlene'. Its magic reflected perfectly the nostalgia for home felt by millions of men and women on both sides of the conflict, and it was undoubtedly *the* song of the 1939-45 war. It wasn't until many years later that I stumbled across the fact that the song had actually been written during the 1914-18 war, by a German soldier, and that 'Lili' and 'Marlene' had been two of his girlfriends.

Four days later, on 17 November, only twelve days after my return, the Commando received the long rumoured and hoped-for orders: 'Return to UK – via Algiers.' It seemed that even Mount Etna demonstrated pleasure at our news – by bursting forth into a spectacular eruption.

Next morning we were on our way to Syracuse, to embark for North Africa. Hopes were high that it would be not only 'Back to Blighty' but nothing less than 'Home for Christmas'!

16 *Return to the UK*

On the afternoon of 19 November we steamed into the harbour at Bizerta, from whence the little *Cadmus* had sailed for Malta little more than three weeks earlier. There had been a change in plan. Instead of sailing direct to Algiers, the Commando was to complete the journey by rail. We regarded this as no more than a minor setback and comforted ourselves with the thought that a train would surely be much faster than a ship.

Immediately after docking, the Commando filed ashore and marched the short distance to the railway station. Our first sight of the train awaiting us was another jolt. There was no doubt about the vintage of those wagons, each bearing the legend *'40 hommes ou 8 chevaux'* (40 men or 8 horses). All had undoubtedly been well used in World War I, and we were amazed that some were still around to play a part in our World War II. From the lingering odour, we suspected that they had been used more for the horses than the men.

The diminutive engine was of an even greater age. Its cruising speed proved to be of the order of four miles an hour (there was no problem in hopping off to change 'compartments'), and it seemed incapable of speeds of more than about twenty-five miles an hour, even when the gradient was in its favour. Stops were frequent, long and unexplained, and each time the juggernaut screeched to a halt there would be a mad scramble to brew tea. At first we were able to get boiling water from the engine-driver but demand soon outstripped supply and alternative arrangements had to be made. There were empty biscuit tins and unlimited supplies of sand but no petrol, so Benghazi cookers weren't the answer. The solution hit upon was to use the tins to burn wood, and these were dubbed 'Bizerta cookers'. Unfortunately there was very little timber to be scavenged from the sides of the track, so recourse had to be made to utilizing a few non-essential parts of the wagons – we found that the floorboards were easiest to prise loose.

The maddening start/stop/start/stop journey continued throughout the night, and even with the doors closed, the absence of part of the floor made our quarters much too cold and draughty for any serious sleep. Morning, with the welcome warmth of the sun seeping into chilled limbs, brought relief from the night, but there was no relief from the spasmodic progress of the train, which clattered along its lonely track throughout another hot day. Many of the abrupt jangling starts would interrupt a water-boiling session, and as the train was chuffing off, there would be a rush to dangle the fire tins through the holes in the floor or hook them on door handles or any other projection on the outsides of the wagons.

A second miserably cold night was followed by the thawing process of another sunrise, and still we clanked on. It wasn't until late in the afternoon of the third day that our journey squealed to an end and we were ordered to de-train – onto the low platform of a station which was clearly much too small to be Algiers. There was no visible indication of where it might be, and we were told no more than that the Commando would spend the night in a nearby transit camp before completing the journey next day. The fact that movement had stopped was dispiritingly ominous but we reckoned that, after forty-eight hours travelling, there couldn't be very much of the original 400 miles still to cover. As we marched off, however, I caught sight of a station nameplate and goggled in disbelief. During those interminable hours on the train we had covered no more than 120 miles, and they were the very same ones trundled over by the tank-transporter some four weeks earlier – we were in Bône.

In No. 4 Transit Camp accommodation was in large, empty marquees set up on the grubby desert sand. This was appreciably more comfortable as a bed than the floor of a draughty railway wagon but did nothing to ease the nagging 'transit camp feeling'. Next morning, washed, shaved and ready to go, we waited – and waited – and waited. Tins of cold M & V were passed around for lunch, and we were still waiting and wondering, without any explanation. When food for an evening meal was issued, we glumly settled down for our second night in Transit Camp No. 4.

The following day was repetition of the first, and thereafter day followed day without any why or wherefore until all hopes of 'a train tomorrow' had faded completely. It was just as though we had dropped out of the real world into a miserable, aimless and endless Alice in Wonderland existence. The only bright feature of our stay in that camp was a double issue of 'NAAFI rations', the weekly dole-out of cigarettes and chocolate made to everyone in the Services. It was as if Rudyard Kipling's description of a Royal Marine as 'a soldier an' a sailor too' was being taken quite literally. In the camp we were fed and watered by the Army as Ranks in Transit and were entitled to our weekly ration as such. At the same time we received a ration from the local naval stores depot, so cigarettes became the invariable 'chips' for the card schools. After changing hands time and again, they tended to become rather limp and grimy but still smokable – if you won.

There were so few happenings to relieve the monotony of waiting for we knew not what that it was quite an occasion when the local Arab dockworkers went on strike – when they should have been loading an ammunition ship for Italy. The Commando took over their work while they stood glowering from the sidelines. We never learned if the Arabs achieved what they had gone on strike for or whether it was just that marines were effective as strike-breakers. Either way, after only one day the Arabs went back to their work and we went back to our cards.

By the time November had passed into December, it looked as though the Commando had become inexplicably, inextricably and permanently jammed in the military pipeline. The arrival of a new commanding officer, Colonel Grey, flown out from the UK, seemed to make no appreciable difference to our situation. By this time every conceivable rumour about our departure, imminent or otherwise, and for every imaginable theatre of war, had long since been worked to death. We awaited the festive season in an atmosphere of all-pervading, uninterested flatness.

On 23 December the Commando was paraded for an address by our new colonel, and he didn't take long to deliver his message. We were to leave by road next morning – destination, Algiers, where a ship was already waiting to carry us back to the UK! When the parade had been dismissed, No. 4 Transit Camp burst into a whirl of frenetic activity such as it had probably never before experienced. The Commando came to life with an almighty bang. There was little packing to do, so we rushed around buying anything that might serve as souvenirs or Christmas gifts, then filled all vacant kitbag space with oranges, lemons and tangerines – all of which were unobtainable in the UK at that time. The night passed with many of us hardly daring to believe that 41 might really be getting on the move again.

At the parade early next day, the morning of Christmas Eve, there were no latecomers, but not everyone was convinced. Not until a column of beautiful TCVs rolled into camp were the last doubts about our departure dispelled. We scrambled on board like schoolboys at the end of their first term at boarding school. Almost immediately we were on our way, with the convoy rolling through the gates amidst billowing clouds of dust and successive waves of elated cheers.

The champagne fizz of leaving No. 4 quickly evaporated but the ample sufficiency of being once again on the move persisted. Throughout a day of sweaty heat and dust we bounced about on the hard seats and long after the sun had set were still travelling westwards. As the TCVs rumbled on through the star-filled night, we huddled together for warmth in the near-zero temperatures. There was little talking. Some tried to sleep, but most were

probably fully occupied with their own thoughts – of
Christmas Eves they had known in the past or of how they
had been hoping to spend that particular one at home.
It was nearly midnight when the convoy came to a halt.
Freezing cold, sore in the buttocks, cramped and hungry,
we were led to a dilapidated wooden building standing
alone in a bleak mountain wilderness. A semi-ruin, the
large, barn-like structure was already well filled with
hundreds of men. In the middle of the beaten earth floor a
large bonfire flamed and crackled and, despite gaping
holes in the roof acting as chimneys, it was filled with
pungent white woodsmoke. With barely sufficient room
for each man to have a place to sit but warmed by the fire
and our closely packed bodies, breathing the heavy,
smoke-laden air, we dozed intermittently until the early
hours of Christmas morning. Then, shivering in the
pre-dawn darkness, it was back onto the TCVs. As they
rolled on their way again, we remained standing,
stamping our feet and flailing arms around shoulders in
vain efforts to keep warm. Two hours later, when the sun
had climbed back over the hills, there was much more heat
than we wanted.

Late in the morning of Christmas Day, our truck
breasted another in the seemingly endless succession of
desert ridges, but this time we saw a wide panorama of the
Mediterranean stretched before us. A large town, plainly
Algiers, lay scarcely twenty miles away. As the convoy
careered down to the coastal plain, there were spontaneous
cheers and shouts of, 'It won't be long now!' Then, quite
unexpectedly, the TCVs pulled off the road and we
looked at one another questioningly until assured that the
halt was just to have something to eat.

Christmas Day lunch in the armed Services is
traditionally served to the Other Ranks by their
commissioned officers, but on that occasion there was no
tradition and very little lunch. It didn't take long to eat the
corned beef and biscuits plus half a canned pear for
dessert but then came another of those long, unexplained
waits. It was late afternoon before the convoy rolled into
Algiers, the large vehicles spreading alarm and some

chaos amongst the Arab street traders. Then came a further unexpected hold-up when the TCVs deposited us at the city's football stadium where we were to wait to board the ship 'when it was dark'.

After filing into our allotted places we sat in the gathering gloom as more troops by the hundred gradually filled the stands on both sides of the pitch. All that was missing was the football match – until some wag started it off by bawling out, 'Come on, Spurs!' at the top of his voice. The effect was like a Cordtex fuse on a slab of gun cotton. The darkness exploded into a gale of noise, as the entire stadium echoed to the names of practically every team in the English and Scottish football leagues. Groups of supporters chanted their war cries, claimed goals, told the referee to, 'Chuck 'im orf!' and 'Shoot the basket!' There were appeals for offside, allegations of fouls and successive waves of cheers and counter-cheers as imaginary goals came thick and fast. For a full five minutes the uproar continued; then, as abruptly as it had started, the clamour subsided. The fun had fizzled out, the game of 'ghost football' had lost its savour, and a dozing silence settled over the packed stadium once more.

It was very late by the time we were roused and told to 'Get Rigged!' We filed down between the rows of seats and piled onto more trucks waiting for us outside the stadium. A short, subdued drive through the sleeping city, then we debussed once again. This time we really had arrived at a dockside. As we jumped down from the tailboard, there, towering high above our heads, was the huge shadowy bulk of a ship, *our ship!* We tagged on to the end of an untidy string of faceless figures leading to the foot of a steep, narrow gangway, its top lost in the blackness high above our heads. Apart from the overall darkness and the fact that all movement was upwards, that gangway was probably the nearest thing to Jacob's ladder that many of us were likely to come across. A troopship may not be everyone's dream of heaven but, for us, that one came very close.

We shuffled along the quayside foot by foot, dragging our kitbags, heavy with the extra pounds of oranges and lemons. Then came the major effort of climbing the gangway in full equipment with kitbag on one shoulder, rifle slung over the other and still keeping a firm grip on the handrail. The pace being set by those further up was agonizingly slow, and muscles were soon aching to cracking point. Muttered imprecations and coarse pleas to 'get a bloody move on' had no effect. Minds became plagued with visions of kitbags slipping from overstrained fingers and plummeting to the dockside far below, but somehow you managed to hang on and eventually reached the top. With the last stumbling step onto the ship's deck, you could really let the bag drop, with a huge gasp of relief.

The ship was the SS *Otranto*, already packed to overflowing with a trooper's usual heterogeneous collection of uniformed humanity. There were men and women of the land, air and naval forces of Great Britain and some of her Allies, members of various nursing services and a mixed bag of German prisoners. 41 Commando was amongst the last to go aboard. Before dawn on Boxing Day, the ship had been eased away from the quayside.

Our trip home was uneventful. In the early hours of 4 January, 1944 SS *Otranto* nosed her way into the Firth of Clyde. The Commando disembarked at Gourock, where we had taken ship some six months earlier. The wheel had turned full circle.

Appendix I: *A Brief History of the Royal Marines*

The tradition of soldiers serving with the Fleet was brought about by an Order in Council dated 28 October 1664, when, in anticipation of a second war with the Dutch, Charles II sanctioned the formation of a regiment of land soldiers for service with the Navy. A force of 1,200 men was to be raised, divided into six Companies and 'distributed in His Majesty's fleets'. They were put under the command of the Lord High Admiral of England, the Duke of York and Albany, and in consequence were styled 'The Duke of York and Albany's Maritime Regiment of Foot' or 'The Lord High Admiral's Regiment'.

Many of the first recruits came from the recently abolished Trained Bands of London – the militia raised by the City Corporation to defend London against the Parliamentary forces, nicknamed the 'Jollies', and Royal Marines are still, on occasion, referred to by that name. Other men who enlisted in the new regiment had, presumably, been on the opposite side during the Civil War, in Cromwell's army, as both Protestants and Catholics were numbered amongst its officers and men. The men were attracted by a bounty and the expectation of prize money when they were involved in the capture of enemy ships.

These sea soldiers proved their usefulness during the Anglo-Dutch Wars (between 1665 and 1674), and by 1672 they were being styled 'marines', but in 1689 the regiment was disbanded. In 1690, however, during the War of the Grand Alliance (1688-97) King William III authorized the formation of two Marine Regiments, and thereafter new regiments were raised or existing Army regiments were embarked as marines as required. Conversely, when naval strength was reduced, battalions of marines would be re-formed as regiments of the line. On 24 July 1704, during the War of the Spanish Succession (1702-13), marines under Sir George Rooke took possession of the Rock of Gibraltar. For six months thereafter they successfully defended it against the combined forces of Spain and France, 'thus being considered to have gained an immortal honour'. After the Peace of Aix-la-Chapelle in 1748, they were again disbanded, but in 1755 the need for marines was felt once more; they were re-formed and have been in continuous existence ever since.

During the Seven Years' War (1756-63), when the British Fleet was blockading Brest, marines seized Belle Ile as an advanced base for the operation. In recognition of this they were granted the privilege of wearing the victor's traditional laurel wreath on their colours, and this has since been incorporated in their badge.

Unlike seamen who signed on from voyage to voyage, theirs was a long-term engagement, so they brought an element of continuity into the Navy, and this inevitably involved them in the training of sailors to fight at sea. Between 1763 and the start of the French Revolutionary Wars in 1793, marines were in action with the Army in India and throughout all phases of the American War of Independence. During the same period they also fought in all the naval battles of the period, including Cape St Vincent, the Glorious First of June, Martinique, Dogger Bank and the Battle of the Saints, and were even called upon to guard convicts being transported to Botany Bay.

On 29 April 1802, after the conclusion of French Revolutionary Wars, George III granted the marines the style of 'Royal' – 'in consideration of their very meritorious service during the late war'. Later, during the Napoleonic Wars (1803-15) and the war with America (1812-15), marines were involved in many operations, which included the capture of Capetown, Buenos Aires, Montevideo, Washington, New Orleans, Réunion, Mauritius and sundry bases in Uruguay. There were also raids on the Spanish coast and the American coast, particularly in Florida, and a landing on the Dutch island of Walcheren. In addition, they covered the Army re-embarkation at Corunna, were involved in the bombardment of Constantinople and participated in Nelson's victories of the Nile, Copenhagen and Trafalgar.

In 1827 the Duke of Clarence, Lord High Admiral of Great Britain and General of Marines (afterwards William IV), presented the Corps with new colours displaying the badge which every officer and man wears to this day. His Royal Highness explained that, owing to the difficulty of making a selection from 'so many glorious deeds' to inscribe on the colours, their sovereign, George IV, had been pleased to adopt 'the Great Globe itself', circled with laurel, as the most appropriate emblem of a corps whose duties carried them to all parts of the world, 'in every quarter of which they had earned laurels by their valour'. His Majesty considered that his own cipher (GR IV) should be interlaced with the 'Foul Anchor' which showed their connection with the Royal Navy. Their motto *'Per Mare Per Terram'* ('By Sea, By Land'), 'peculiarly their own', remained. Surmounting the Imperial Crown on the badge, His Majesty also directed that the word 'Gibraltar' should appear in commemoration of their earliest distinction.

The role of the Royal Marines was, traditionally, to reinforce the strength of the Navy, and from 1804 a marine's main duty at sea was with the ship's guns. Marines remained the Navy's gunnery instructors until 1859, when continuous service for seamen was instituted. At about that time too, the Corps was re-organized into the Royal Marine Artillery (RMA – Blue Marines) and the Royal Marine Light Infantry (RMLI – Red Marines). Thereafter, until the 1950s, marines continued to man a proportion of the main and secondary armament of all the larger warships of the Royal Navy, although the distinction between RMA and RMLI had been abandoned in 1923. The marine's quarters on board ship – always referred to as 'the Marine Barracks' – were invariably located as an intentional buffer between the officers' quarters and the crew's mess deck, as they were more likely to remain loyal in the event of a mutiny by the pressganged seamen.

An early additional role for Royal Marines, ashore and afloat was the provision of marine bands for all major naval occasions, which led to the institution of the Royal Marine School of Music. Royal Marine Barracks fly the Union Jack and not the White Ensign because, although under the control of the Admiralty (through the Headquarters of the Commandant-General Royal Marines), they are not commissioned as ships like naval shore establishments – generally referred to as 'stone frigates'. Marines are paid by the Admiralty and whilst afloat come under the Naval Discipline Act; ashore, however, they come under the Army Act, and the dividing line is the ship's gangway.

At the time of the Napoleonic Wars the Corps had a strength of around 30,000 men but its numbers were reduced to almost a token force during the next twenty-five years of comparative peace, and then it fluctuated between 10,000 and 20,000 for the rest of the nineteenth century according to the needs of the various campaigns in which it was involved. There was no shortage of them – from the Carlist Wars in Spain in the late 1830s to the operations in West Africa of 1892-1900. They were in action in Syria and China, in India during the Mutiny, in the Crimean War, Burma, New Zealand, Abyssinia, Ashanti, Zululand, Japan, Egypt and the Sudan.

During the First World War the Corps strength rose to 50,000 men and, in addition to their significant role on ships of the line, where they suffered very heavy losses, they were also involved in many actions ashore. They fought as artillerymen (heavy artillery in West Africa, howitzer brigades and anti-aircraft batteries in France and elsewhere) and as infantrymen and raiding forces – with the Naval Division on the Western Front and the Dardanelles, in Serbia, Egypt and the Aegean, at Zeebrugge, then as rearguard in the 1918 retreat and, even after the Armistice, in North Russia. Throughout the war they exemplified their dual role of sea soldiers.

In the Second World War, the marines carried on the tradition in all parts of the world. At sea they still manned about a third of the main and secondary armament of all battleships and cruisers. On land they were busy from the Norway campaign, through the Dieppe and other raids on 'Fortress Europe', the defence of Singapore, river actions in Burma, raids on the Arakan coast, landings in the Mediterranean, at Tobruk, and in Sicily, Italy, Albania and Yugoslavia, as well as at Myebon and Kangaw in the Far East. They provided anti-aircraft batteries in the UK. Marine Commandos by the thousand went ashore on D-Day and helped hold the beachhead, then went forward with the Allied Armies and later (together with Army Commandos) opened the way to Antwerp by the landings on Walcheren and South Beveland. They were active in the Maas River operations, took part in the crossings of the Rhine and then carried on into Germany.

Marines also extended their areas of expertise. They formed complete 'packages' for the defence of naval bases: artillery, land and anti-aircraft, searchlights, transport, signals, engineers, infantry – these were the MNBDOs (Mobile Naval Base Defence Organizations), one of which carried out an invaluable rearguard action to cover the withdrawal of Allied troops from Crete after the German airborne assault; they formed 'Light Boat Squadrons' whose canoeists made the famous 'Cockleshell Heroes' raid on Bordeaux, and a battery of the Armoured Support Group, equipped with Centaur tanks, went ashore on D-Day. Royal Marine pilots flew with the Fleet Air Arm; Royal Marine Engineers constructed naval air stations and bases for the fleet; marines manned and operated landing-craft for close-in artillery and rocket support for amphibious operations; many marine commandos volunteered for parachute training.

The most important and lasting feature of their operations in the Second World War, however, would appear to be the concentration upon the Commando system of infantry assault. With the phasing-out of large capital ships in favour of either aircraft or missile forms of attack, sea-borne artillery, with some minor exceptions, has outlived its usefulness. Nevertheless, there has been no change in the basic fact that no enemy position can be 'occupied' other than by men on the ground moving around on their own two feet. Present-day marines are just as likely to appear before the enemy from the air – by helicopter or parachute – as from the sea, but the men are still very much as Rudyard Kipling saw them a hundred years ago:

> ... a-doin' all kinds o' things,
> Like landin' 'isself with a Gatlin' gun to talk to them 'eathen kings.

Since the Second World War they haven't been idle. They have served with the Rhine Flotilla and as UN protection forces in Haifa, Tripoli and Benghazi, covered the final withdrawals from Palestine and the Canal Zone, fought in the Korean War, were engaged in anti-terrorist operations in Cyprus, played a major part in the 1956 Suez landings and served in Hong Kong, Northern Ireland, Kenya, Tanganyika, Kuwait, Aden and Borneo. To quote Kipling again, '... they ain't no limpin' procrastitutes'. Since 1972 the marines have had a continuing NATO commitment alongside the Norwegians on Europe's northern flank, patrolling and exercising in the remote mountainous regions beyond the Arctic Circle where they are moved and supplied by their own air squadron of helicopters. There they also parachute to secret rendezvous in the snows, ski 25 km in a day with 30 kg loads and sleep in two-man snow holes. It is little wonder then that in 1982, when the need arose to prise the Falkland Islands from the grip of an invader, the Royal Marines were in the van of the assault.

To this day, there's not a 'Royal' ('Jolly', 'Bootneck', 'Leatherneck' – call him what you will) who won't agree with Kipling that:

> There isn't a job on the top o' the earth the beggar don't know, or do,

You can leave 'im at night on a bald man's head to paddle 'is own canoe.

E's a sort of bloomin' cosmopolouse – soldier an' sailor too

– and be prepared to put his neck on the line to prove it.

Sources

The Story of the Royal Marines (NAAFI Print, 1935); *The Royal Marines – The Admiralty Account of Their Achievement, 1939-1943* (HMSO, 1944) and (J. D. Ladd) *Royal Marine Commando* (Hamlyn, 1982).

Appendix II: *Muster-Roll of 7 Section, Q Troop, 41 Royal Marines Commando*

The following muster-roll for the time of the Sicily Landing, 10 July 1943, was compiled by L/Cpl 'Jock' More, to whom the author is greatly indebted for its reproduction, and with whom the first contact since the war was made only after an article had appeared in The Sunday Post, *in February 1988, seeking information about the family of Alec Kennedy.*

Section Commander:
Lieut. Peter H. Haydon — Wounded Salerno, killed Walcheren

Section Sergeant:
Sgt. Ken Shepherd — (In hospital at time of Salerno)
Cpl. Jack ('Ginger') Carlisle
Cpl. Tommy Carr — Killed in Belgium
Cpl. George ('Jan') Maley — (acting Section Sgt. at Salerno)
Cpl. Ted ('Buck') Taylor — Wounded D-Day
L/Cpl. Bill ('Jock') More
L/Cpl. Bobby Mortlock
L/Cpl. George ('Simmo') Simpson — Wounded in Holland
Mne. Evan Bath
Mne. Bill Blackwell
Mne. Bob Brown — Wounded Salerno, killed D-Day
Mne. Harold Colloff — Wounded Salerno
Mne. Mick Donovan
Mne Jimmy Godin
Mne. Ronnie Green — Wounded Salerno
Mne. Jack Horsfield
Mne. Derek Johnson
Mne. Alec Kennedy — Killed Salerno
Mne. Bill McClaren
Mne. Alec McClelland
Mne. George McDougall
Mne. Bill Marshall — Battle exhaustion Salerno, wounded Walcheren

Mne. Ray ('Mitch') Mitchell	Wounded Salerno
Mne. Tom Mitchell	Wounded Salerno, wounded D-Day
Mne. John Read	
Mne. Alec Shaw	Wounded Salerno, wounded D-Day
Mne. Ted Shine	
Mne. Bill Smith	Wounded D plus 1
Mne. Bill ('Geordie') Swindale	Killed D-Day
Mne. Harry Weiss	

Index